PSYCHOLOGICAL THERAPIES IN PRIMARY CARE

Training and Training Standards

Edited by
Douglas Hooper and Philippa Weitz

KARNAC
LONDON NEW YORK

First published in 2006 by
H. Karnac (Books) Ltd.
6 Pembroke Buildings, London NW10 6RE

British Library Cataloguing in Publication Data

A C.I.P. for this book is available from the British Library

ISBN10: 1 85575 491 6
ISBN13: 978 1 85575 491 1

Edited, designed, and typeset by RefineCatch Ltd, Bungay, Suffolk
Printed in Great Britain

www.karnacbooks.com

The editors would like to dedicate this book to Graham Curtis-Jenkins. It is the tireless pioneering work carried out with such enthusiasm and professionalism by Graham that has given the counselling in primary counselling care profession its solid roots.

CONTENTS

CONTRIBUTORS

Christine Driscoll has a background in development gained from working as a clinician, manager, educator and organisational development facilitator.

She has experience in setting up systems – for example in quality, clinical leadership and clinical supervision. She has recently run a project across Kent, Surrey and Sussex to improve appraisal in Primary Care – this included designing and delivering training and development with GP tutors, primary care tutors, GPs and PCT leads for appraisal and personal development planning.

Currently she works independently with a mixed portfolio that includes facilitating and offering supervision to individuals and groups of senior nurses and managers. She also contributes to developing effective systems for reflective practice including: supervision and facilitation training in clinical supervision; mentoring; personal development planning; and developmental appraisal in a variety of organisational settings including secondary care, primary care, and voluntary and charity organisations.

JOHN EATOCK is Lead Advisor for Healthcare Counselling and Psychotherapy at the British Association for Counselling and Psychotherapy.

JOAN FOSTER is Chair of the National Association of Counsellors and Psychotherapists in Primary Care (CPC). She has worked as a Primary Care Counsellor since 1992. She also works as a trainer in time-limited counselling and supervision and runs a number of training courses for CPC. In addition, she acts as consultant to a number of PCG/Ts in the establishment and running of primary care counselling services and is involved in interview panels and in evaluation of services.

As Chair of CPC, Joan was a member of the Department of Health, Workforce Action Team, Primary Care Sub-Group addressing the Workforce Planning, Education and Training Issues for Adult Mental Health Services.

She has published a paper on "Counselling in primary care and the new NHS" in the *British Journal of Guidance and Counselling*, 28(2), (2000). She is joint author, with Peter Bower, of *"Quality in Counselling in Primary Care": A Guide for Effective Commissioning and Clinical Governance* (National Primary Care Research and Development Centre, 2001) and of *Psychological Therapies in Primary Care – Setting up a Managed Service* (London: Karnac, 2005).

PENNY HENDERSON is an independent counselling practitioner and supervisor based in Cambridge. As teacher and consultant she has been involved in developing syllabuses for psychological therapy in primary care for a number of years.

EMERITUS PROFESSOR DOUGLAS HOOPER is Chair of the Counselling and Psychotherapy Forum for Primary Care. He is a clinical and counselling psychologist and has had a particular interest in the development of counselling services. A former President of the British Association for Counselling and Psychotherapy, he has recently been much involved in the development of psychological therapies in Primary Care.

MICHAEL JACOBS is Visiting Professor at the Institute of Health and Community Studies at Bournemouth University, and is author of a number of key texts used in psychodynamic and general counselling training.

STEVE JOHNSON has specialised in professional liability insurance since 1988 when, together with a colleague, he launched a Professional Liability Insurance scheme for members of the British Psychological Society. The scheme grew quickly and soon expanded into areas surrounding psychology, particularly counselling and psychotherapy. Steve is a regular attendee at various conferences held by the major professional bodies and was a founder member of the Counselling and Psychotherapy Forum for Primary Care.

MAUREEN MOORE is a Registered Integrative Psychotherapist and Director of Qualifications Development at the Counselling and Psychotherapy Central Awarding Body. She has been a coordinator for a Primary Care Counselling Service and a provider of Clinical Supervision for Counsellors in Primary Care and in Independent Practice. Maureen's background in nursing, health visiting and community health promotion led to teaching in Further Education where she was responsible for development and delivery of Adult Education, Counselling and Access Programmes. She has extensive experience of working for the NHS in the community, in Primary Care and in Acute Psychiatric Hospital settings. She has a specialist interest in working with trauma and stress management. She has presented workshops and lectures on Wellbeing and Health in Retirement for public and private organisations.

ANTONIA MURPHY is a graduate in Psychodynamic Counselling from the WPF. Following her move to Nottingham in 1993, she continued to work as a Counsellor in Primary Care and subsequently as Co-ordinator of the SDHA counselling service from 1995–2002 which contributed to her growing knowledge of the work of the therapist in general practice. Her concern for the provision of best practice in Counselling and Psychotherapy in Primary Care nationally has been further developed in her role as Vice Chair of CPC (the Association of Counsellors and Psychotherapists in Primary Care). Antonia is a BACP Accredited/Registered Practitioner, and a CPC Registered Member and Supervisor Member.

Tim O'Brien is a Lead Manager with ENTO, an independent organisation which develops occupational standards for various occupations, commissioned by the Government. He has acted as Senior Consultant for the Development of National Occupational Standards in Counselling.

Jane Rosoman is Chair of the Network of Primary Care Counselling Providers in the NHS, and Head of Service for Primary Care Counselling at Ealing PCT.

Naomi Stewart is a Consultant Adult Psychotherapist who has over 15 years experience as a therapist and trainer. She has worked extensively as a supervisor, consultant and trainer in both the NHS and primary care, and is a member of the UKCP Training Standards Committee with a particular interest in supervision.

Professor André Tylee is Professor of Primary Care Mental Health in the Institute of Psychiatry at Kings College London, and also Chair of the Primary Care Programme at the National Institute of Mental Health Education in England (NIMHE).

Philippa Weitz is Executive Director of the Counselling and Psychotherapy Forum for Primary Care, with over 20 years experience of training and delivery of Continuing Professional Development within mental health, with specialist interests in primary care counselling and bereavement. She is trained as a psychological counsellor and a teacher.

AN A–Z OF ORGANISATIONS AND THEIR ACRONYMS

BACP	British Association for Counselling and Psychotherapy
BAPPS	British Association of Psychoanalytic and Psychodynamic Supervisors
BCP	British Psychoanalytic Council
BPS	British Psychological Society
CMHT	Community mental health team
CMS	Counselling in Medical Settings Division, now the FHCP
CORE	Clinical Outcomes for Routine Evaluation (a complex set of audit materials relating to client outcomes)
CPC	The Association of Counsellors and Psychotherapists in Primary Care
CPCAB	Counselling and Psychotherapy Central Awarding Body
CPCT	Counselling in Primary Care Trust
ENTO	Committed to developing the competence of people

	who work with people through the use of National Occupational Standards (NOS)
FHCP	Faculty for Healthcare Counsellors and Psychotherapists (a division of BACP)
Forum	The Counselling and Psychotherapy Forum for Primary Care
HPC	Health Professions Council
NICE	National Institute for Clinical Excellence
NIMHE	National Institute of Mental Health Education in England
NSP	Network of Service Providers
NVQ	National Vocational Qualifications
PARN	Professional Associations Research Network
PCG	Primary care group (now defunct)
PCT	Primary care trust
QAA	Quality Assurance Agency for Higher Education
QCA	Qualifications and Curriculum Authority
UKCP	United Kingdom Council for Psychotherapy

PREFACE

Representing the Patients' Interests

As a general practitioner from 1980 to 2001, I witnessed the growth of counselling in primary care. In my own surgery, we had a volunteer counsellor from Relate in the early 1980s but soon progressed to having both a counselling psychologist and a clinical psychologist when we held our own budget. Most of this resource was subsequently spread throughout the primary care trust (PCT) and centralised, with advantages and disadvantages to both us and our patients. A distinct advantage is that the service is now professionally managed, with clear quality standards and monitoring of patient outcome, as well as the provision of high-class training and supervision for the counsellors.

Patients referred to counselling services are often in a vulnerable state and need rigorous protection as well as care. There has been a steady improvement in defining and adhering to quality standards by the counselling profession over the past decade or two and this is readily apparent from this book. I was privileged to have been a Trustee of the Counselling in Primary Care Trust

(CPCT) to advise Dr Graham Curtis-Jenkins on his valiant and pioneering work in this area. I was also privileged to see the birth and growth of CPC under the leadership of Joan Foster, with the assistance again of Dr Curtis-Jenkins. As a GP interested in primary care mental health, I now watch the current Department of Health programme to increase the provision of psychological therapies with great interest. Through largely consumer pressure and recent National Institute for Clinical Evidence guidelines it is increasingly apparent that counselling services need to be greatly increased, and this of course will have a great impact on training provision. It will be necessary to increase training provision without sacrificing quality.

A challenge for the future is for training to engender a greater degree of multiprofessional working in the area of primary care mental health. There are an increasing number of other primary care mental health professionals, such as the new graduate primary care mental health workers, gateway workers and a range of workers in NHS walk-in centres. Working in a 'primary care mental health team' will become more and more commonplace and a growing number of GPs or nurses with special interests in mental health will be part of such teams, which often include mental health professionals from nursing or psychology backgrounds. In addition, national guidance on conditions such as depression increasingly involves a 'stepped care approach' with a clear role for counsellors.

An uncommon but important role for counsellors can be that of supporting their colleagues, particularly those who still have no tradition of peer supervision. Some of these contextual issues are rapidly changing and may change further with future iterations of the General Medical Services contract and provision for 'enhanced services'. Counsellors, like all primary care professionals, need to keep abreast of such changes and often the opportunities they bring for innovative practice and services. A particular challenge for the self-employed counsellor who often goes into a practice for a session each week is to become a valued part of a multiprofessional team, with all the networking this involves. It seems a great shame to me that in my experience most of the new graduate primary care workers aspire to become clinical psychologists in mental health services rather than counsellors, counselling psychologists or psychotherapists working in primary care settings. This presumably reflects an inequity in status and in my opinion needs remedying for the future of primary care counselling. Those responsible for maintaining standards in training also need to address this issue in order to encourage their young colleagues to join them.

Professor André Tylee
Professor of Primary Care Mental Health
King's College London at the Institute of Psychiatry
Chair, Primary Care Programme of the National Institute of Mental Health Education in England (NIMHE)

Introduction

Douglas Hooper and Philippa Weitz

PRIMARY care counselling is in its ascendancy. Primary care counsellors now have their place on the NHS pay spine, and they are established as practitioners in their own right with professional body representation within Counsellors and Psychotherapists in Primary Care (CPC), the Faculty of Healthcare (BACP) and the new Psychotherapeutic Counselling Section within UKCP. Remembering that primary care counsellors come from a wider variety of professional backgrounds, the authors are acutely aware that their training may not entirely qualify primary care counsellors for the work that they do.

This book looks in turn at the elements that need to be considered in order to create a framework to take this important training forward. Therefore the chapters cover the history of counselling in primary care, the politics behind recent developments, the research background to this service, the NHS organisation of counselling and psychological therapies, the training programmes and the proposed basic training requirements, and the important issues of mentoring and supervision. These are all matters that, in our view, go to make up what is required to ensure that the primary care counsellor can carry out his or her role to the highest standard.

We believe that counsellors and psychological therapists must provide quality care for patients, clients or service users at their initial point of entry to the health service – namely in the primary care general practice setting. This is where the majority of patients, clients and service users are and wish to be treated. As all kinds of health care move to the community rather than the hospital site, each GP practice will become more complex and multi-disciplinary.

One result of this complexity is an increasing number of health professionals using the site, although not many of those will be concerned with mental health issues. But among the mental health professionals it is most important that the perennial turf wars are not allowed to proliferate. This is less likely to happen if counsellors are secure in their own identity and have been competently trained to understand and engage with other colleagues. Sometimes the psychological therapy community has been disdainful of the so-called medical model of health and illness, retreating into the laager of the pure psyche. We believe that, properly educated and trained, the primary care counsellor will enable, not disable, his or her colleagues to understand their daily problems in new ways.

We realise that we are demanding a good deal of resources for the proper training we outline here, but we also believe that this investment will yield quite disproportionate results, and that the authors of these pages will contribute significantly to providing more and better mental health care.

Finally, what we, the editors, had in mind behind this book is that the only 'fit for purpose' courses provided are those few externally validated. This is via either QAA[1] or QCA,[2] together with externally validated university courses, which leaves us with a huge melting pot in between of private training providers (ranging from excellent to very poor). Joan Foster's Chapter One demonstrates that this arose because counselling is currently unregulated, with no grants for students. The challenge for training providers is to move to fit-for-purpose, externally validated training appropriate for the 90 per cent of patients, clients and service users using the primary care mental health services of the twenty-first century NHS.

Notes

1 The Quality Assurance Agency for Higher Education www.qaa.ac.uk
2 Qualifications and Curriculum Authority www.qca.org.uk

Part I

The Field: History, Need and Provision

CHAPTER ONE

The History of Primary Care Counselling

Joan Foster

Introduction

THIS chapter describes the development of primary care counselling in the National Health Service in England, Wales and Scotland. In addition it explores the processes that took place in this development. It endeavours to give a deeper understanding of the spectacular increase in numbers of primary care counsellors over the past 35 years, the speed at which this has taken place and the dynamics that have resulted.

Background

Historically 'counsellors first started working in primary general practice in the late 1960s, and by 1992, 31% of English and Welsh practices reported having a counsellor on site' (Addington-Hall et al., 1993; Burton et al., 2001). Let us pause there for a minute: who were these counsellors? Many of the counsellors working in primary care from the late 1960s to the early 1980s were Relate (then Marriage Guidance) counsellors. Certainly my first experience of receiving counselling was in a GP surgery with a Marriage Guidance counsellor in 1985. The first reference to 'practice counsellors' was made in 1975 (Barr and Marsh, 1975), and described marriage guidance counselling in a group practice. This being the case, Relate was organisationally thinking futuristically by placing its counsellors in a venue that clients would find non-threatening and convenient. It is also worth mentioning that Relate offered 'couples counselling'. This demonstrates the developing awareness of a psychosocial factor in individual well-being and began the introduction of a new way of thinking about patients in the medical context. This then was the beginning of one of the most fascinating issues that has emerged from primary care counselling – the holistic model in conjunction with the medical model. Regrettably I do not know whether there was any awareness in those early days of the profound consequences of introducing a different approach to well-being into the NHS. I would imagine not to any great extent, but in fact those early developments have been part of major changes in approaches to the treatment of patients.

It is important to acknowledge the work of Michael and Enid Balint in the 1960s, focusing on the patient and exploring an emotional understanding of working as clinicians with the NHS. Their work resulted in new ways of thinking for GPs, with Balint groups being used by GPs to explore their own anxieties and difficulties in their work within their practice and with their patients. The Balint groups resulted in different thinking and approaches for those who participated, incorporating a holistic approach and challenging the defences used by many practitioners to protect themselves from the pain they dealt with day by day. Thus there was some fertile ground for the introduction of psychotherapeutic thinking and interventions within the NHS.

There is also the relevance of the social, economic and political thinking of the late 1960s when counselling was in its infancy in the NHS and as it has developed to date. In a survey of counsellors in 1998 it was discovered that the average counsellor was white (97 per cent) and female (87 per cent), with a mean age of 48.1 years (Burton et al., 2001). If we adopt that as a general truth then those delivering counselling in the 1960s and 1970s would have lived through the Second World War, while the so-called sixties generation would have been working in the 1980s and 1990s. In addition the vast majority of counsellors have come to counselling as a second career. Life experience is still seen to be of value in this profession.

It is also of relevance to bear in mind that society was changing in terms of the rise of feminism and for many there was an attempt to turn away from the Thatcherite view that there is no such thing as society and that individuals have to help themselves. This resulted in counsellors choosing to work within the system (the NHS) in a caring role, to help those in need. However, I consider there were other elements at work; these included a desire to change the system and to receive recognition by the NHS. In addition it is possible that there was a need to belong, to be an insider, not an outsider. It is of importance that we all look at our own motives to understand what place we were attempting to create for counsellors in the NHS.

We therefore have a group of counsellors most of whom have taken up counselling as a second career, working in the NHS. Many of these counsellors were pioneers, the first counsellor in their surgery, coming from the voluntary/private sector. They were self-employed, and often isolated from the primary health care team. They all believed passionately in the effectiveness of the counselling they could offer. The vast majority were trained to offer 'open-ended' counselling and struggled to adapt to limitations imposed upon them. These limitations concerned the number of sessions counsellors could offer to patients and the fact that decisions were made by non-clinicians driven by funding issues and also possibly the need to maintain control.

Working to a Time Limit

The reasons for the development of short-term counselling in primary care are of interest. The evidence suggests that whether an intervention is open-ended or time-limited, the average number of hours per counselling intervention will be 5.9 hours. We can speculate that was a factor in the decision by many health authorities in the 1990s to impose a limit of six hours per counselling intervention. However, it is equally possible that faced with the theoretical possibility of counsellors seeing clients for months or years, some sort of control was deemed essential and six was as good a number as any. We have to ask what clinical knowledge base was used for this decision. In addition, why did the counsellors (and I include myself) accept it? It would seem that there were issues of power and control and that as individuals, with no knowledge of what was happening for others, the counsellors accepted the rules. This was combined with a need 'to belong' and be accepted in the medical world. Indeed in the medical world, six sessions lasting 50 minutes each is a very long time in comparison to the average GP appointment of seven minutes.

There is, then, a situation when professionals are being 'told' what to do with, in their view, no justification for the rule, and having to alter their practice to fit. There is also the fact that individuals do not fit into neat boxes and one person may need five hours, another may need nine and yet another may need two. The results of this have been interesting. First, there has been pressure from individual counsellors and their professional bodies that they should be given the responsibility as professionals to decide the appropriate number of hours a client will require. Moreover, counsellors are trained to work long term and there is often a feeling that they are short-changing their client, or they are not doing the job properly.

Concurrently, in the 1990s there was the development of models of working to a time limit with clients. James Mann and Steve de Schazer were leaders of this in the United States, with others, and this was brought to the UK and further explored and developed. What is of note is that simultaneously, all over the UK, individual primary care counsellors were developing their own skills and practice to meet this requirement of working to a time limit. What is even more interesting is that individually these counsellors developed very similar techniques. So we now have a situation where limits that were imposed for possibly non-clinical reasons are being embraced as a positive development in clinical practice. There are many who believe wholeheartedly in the effectiveness of a time-limited counselling intervention, while not losing their belief in the validity of longer-term work for those who have more complex problems.

Growth of Primary Care Counselling

Traditionally the growth of primary care counselling has been on an individual basis. It is estimated that, in 1999, 60 per cent of counsellors were self-employed, 30 per cent were employed and 10 per cent were volunteers or students. Many of these counsellors were offered self-employed contracts by fund-holding GP surgeries. This is a reflection of the one-to-one nature of the work. Fund-holding surgeries were encouraged to 'go it alone' and the self-employed counsellor found a place in those practices that were more 'psychologically minded' and could see the need for a primary care counsellor as part of the team. In addition there were other motivations, described by Mary Burton: 'One motivation of GPs in employing a practice counsellor has been an attempt to avoid the long waiting lists for clinical psychology, psychiatry and psychotherapy at the secondary level. ... Another motivation to employ counsellors has been cost containment, because practice counsellors' sessional fees tend to be lower than those of clinical psychologists or psychiatrists' (Burton, 1998, p. 10).

This growth was also in recognition of the enormous number of patients presenting with mental health problems in primary care. The National Service Framework for Mental Health in England states: 'Generally, for every one hundred individuals that consult their GP with a mental health problem, nine will be referred to specialist services for assessment and advice, or for treatment' (Department of Health, 1999, p. 3). That means that GPs, primary care counsellors, some CPNs and primary care based psychologists are responsible for the other 91! In addition, Jan Wiener and Mannie Sher state that 'Whilst GPs recognise that as many as 70% of the problems with which patients present have an emotional component, in reality the structure of primary care makes it difficult to deal adequately with emotional distress' (Sher and Wiener, 1998). They argue that there is a changing role of the GP from the single-handed practitioner, who could work holistically with the patient, to a group practice with a more organised approach to service provision. In addition families were now being viewed from a systemic approach and the possibility of working with the 'whole' person was becoming more difficult. Mary Burton confirms the danger of ignoring the 'whole person' when she says: 'GPs who listen only for physical symptoms, ignoring the psychological overlay in the consultation, are at risk of missing significant emotional disorder' (Burton, 1998, p. 3).

The context in which primary care counselling undertook its most dramatic growth – the 1990s – was also one of changes in the structure within which the counsellor was to work, particularly with the take-up of fund-holding. These changes were further compounded by the abolition of fund-holding in 1999 and the introduction of primary care commissioning. This development led to a totally different way of thinking within primary care in England, to be followed by Wales, Scotland and Northern Ireland.

In brief, the individual GP had become in many cases part of a group practice. These group practices then became part of a primary care group (PCG) on 1 April 1999. A PCG usually had a population of about 100,000 and all the GP surgeries within the

PCG had to work together with a PCG board, chief executive and staff. The government thinking was to abolish postcode prescribing and ensure equity of provision across the whole of the PCG. By 1 April 2003, all PCGs had become primary care trusts (PCTs) – 481 PCGs replaced by 302 PCTs. A PCT is a legal body and is able to employ staff.

What was happening to primary care counsellors during this period of enormous change? In a nutshell, their world changed totally. The day of independent self-employed counsellors working in their own surgeries with their private supervisors was over. The reason was three small words in the NHS Plan published in 1998: 'equity of access' (Department of Health, 1998). 'Equity of Access' meant that if one practice offered a service in the PCG/T then they all had to. As there were counsellors in 51 per cent of GP surgeries (Burton et al., 2001), this instantly created a very major problem. How did you spread 51 per cent over 100 per cent without either reducing services or putting in more money?

What was more complex was that, back in 1998, very few in the counselling world recognised this as an issue, and I would suggest even fewer in the then new PCGs. This was because of one fundamental problem faced by primary care counsellors: as far as the NHS was concerned they did not exist. Counsellors, psychotherapists and psychologists are not statutorily regulated and at the time there was no recognised pay spine for counsellors or psychotherapists within the NHS.

I find the dynamics of this fascinating. There have been randomised controlled trials into the efficacy of counselling. The Department of Health (2001) published *Treatment Choice in Psychological Therapies and Counselling*, but we were not listed as a profession anywhere in the NHS. The first mention was in the Department of Health's Primary Care Key Group of the Workforce Action Team considering 'the action required to ensure the primary care workforce is equipped to deal with mental health problems'. The report states the following: 'However, we do consider that terms and conditions of employment, salary and management arrangements should be implemented for counsellors in primary care consistent with the guidance on general NHS employment arrangements' (Mental Health NSF, 2001).

At the time of writing, November 2005, the Department of Health has introduced 'Agenda for Change'[1] and the Knowledge, Skills Framework for all professions working in the NHS. All jobs are evaluated and matched against a pay band and pay spine. Counsellors have been evaluated at national level and the following profiles agreed:

Entry Level Counsellor	Pay Band 5	£18,114–23,442
Counsellor	Pay Band 6	£21,630–29,302
Specialist Counsellor	Pay Band 7	£26,106–34,417

These figures are for 2005, and will be subject to change for 2006 onwards. Discussions are still taking place to evaluate management level posts, which are estimated to be at Bands 8/9.

This is the most important step forward for counsellors because for the first time their existence in the NHS is recognised and they can be counted. Until now they have been a hidden resource, self-employed or paid on Administrative and Clerical or Nursing Grades.

Returning to provision, the National Primary Care Research and Development Centre Tracker Survey of Primary Care Groups and Trusts 2000/2001 (University of Manchester) demonstrated the following PCG/PCT provision of primary care counselling services:

- continue existing provision and/or move to a PCG/T wide service, 73.6%;
- under discussion, 12.5%;
- not on agenda/no agreed policy, 2.8%;
- no primary care counselling provision, 6.9%;
- missing data, 4.2%.

So, we can, with some confidence, state that primary care counselling has arrived and is firmly established in the NHS, even though it is still very much 'the new kid on the block'. Expansion has taken place in many areas, with new money being put in; in others the money has been spread more thinly and there are areas where counselling is being withdrawn. In the transition to managed counselling services there has been a change from a traditional structure of counsellors being paid per clinical hour, to a much more complex structure including pay for supervision, attendance at meetings, note-keeping and administration. In addition there have been battles as to who should manage the primary care counselling service, as reflected in the following points:

> Some clinical psychologists, perceiving the growth of primary care counsellors as a threat to their service contracts with GPs, have attempted to co-opt the fledgling profession into their own departments. ... Competition for the primary care market has become an important issue in the NHS, but some of the divisiveness which has results should be understood in terms of the social defences that come into play when clinicians are required to devote part of their time and energy to marketing their services to purchasers. As Hinshelwood (1996) has pointed out, two kinds of anxiety are operating in this situation. 'Clinical' anxiety results from long-term exposure to the anxieties that have overwhelmed patients. 'Market' anxiety is about the survival of jobs and professions in the internal market. (Burton, 1998, pp. 12, 13)

Why Fight the Battle?

A question we could pause and consider here is: 'why are we so desperate to establish counselling within the NHS?' Organisations such as the British Association of Counselling and Psychotherapy (BACP) and the Association of Counsellors and Psychotherapists in Primary Care (CPC), who came into being in 1998 to ensure the survival of primary care counselling, continually fight to ensure counsellors are appropriately paid, have good conditions of service, are properly managed etc. All of this is absolutely laudable, but the question to ponder is: why do we want to be inside a system that we are often in conflict with? And we should bear in mind the language we use: 'battle, fight, conflict'.

The starting point would have to be: were there alternatives? The answer is yes: counselling could have developed as a 'complementary therapy'. Equally it could have continued in the voluntary sector and in the private sector. The drive for counselling to become part of mainstream NHS provision is worthy of understanding. There seem to have been a number of factors:

- The majority of counsellors working in the NHS were being paid (albeit on very varying rates).
- Counselling was being attacked in the media.
- There was a strong demand to provide talking therapies for mental illness as opposed to drug treatments. As described by Pietroni and Vaspe (2000): 'that counselling is indirectly cost effective, that "talking through" a problem is preferable to symptomatic relief through mechanical, chemical, bureaucratic or draconian means and is likely to be a longer lasting solution'.
- There was a desire to counteract the stigma that mental ill-health was shameful.
- There was a desire to demedicalise the human condition.
- Where counselling was firmly established in primary care it was, on the whole, viewed very positively by the primary health care team.
- A passionate belief in counselling *per se* as an effective therapeutic tool.

What a task we set ourselves! Our allies were the GPs. Their conditions were changing, the time per patient was reduced to 5–10 minutes, and they were increasingly aware 'that patients now expect their GPs to provide some kind of psychological help when they are in distress' (Sher and Wiener, 1998). Concurrently the funding for mental health services in the NHS remained inadequate (it was historically regarded as a Cinderella service). Consequently, many patients who would have been seen in secondary services where now re-referred to primary care – to an overstretched GP whose resources were medication, the practice counsellor (if they had one) or the voluntary sector. This reflects another area of conflict within the NHS – between primary and secondary care mental health services for resources.

Counsellors brought a strong belief in the necessity of boundaries into the NHS, not a culture I would suggest that has a very long suit in such concepts! Counsellors have worked hard not to compromise their standards and though sometimes this has been difficult to say the least, some understanding has been reached in individual surgeries. For example, there is respect for the patient in the sense of no interruptions and being on time, or the need for two equal comfortable chairs rather than a luxurious, leather chair and a hard, plastic one. As understanding deepened, some counsellors were allocated a room, which could be furnished in a different style from a doctor's consulting room. It is also worth noting that counsellors provide a reminder of what was prized but has often been lost by the healing professions: time and space, a special relationship and the emotional element in the process of healing. This could, of course, result in envy from harassed practice staff.

The issue of confidentiality is one that has exercised primary care counsellors greatly. There is an art in working as part of a primary health care team and disclosing information that is relevant and of use to the client, when appropriate. That does not mean disclosing personal information that is not relevant. Again, our inherent respect for the client and approach to confidentiality may be hoped to increase confidentiality levels. However, we have to be aware of the context in which we work: it is not private practice and we are working as part of a team. The counsellor who provides no feedback to the referrer will not help the client or help the cause of counselling. Transparency will help understanding of the work we do.

Change

Integration within the mainstream comes at a price. The major result has been the end of the self-employed counsellor working in isolation in a GP surgery. Today, all PCTs have moved or are moving to a managed service approach. This takes varying forms but the inevitable consequence is that the counsellor now has to work as a member of a team, to guidelines and protocols set by others. It is to be hoped that this is a consultative process but that is not always the case.

Over the past two to three years, the primary care counsellor has had to tolerate a working environment of uncertainty and change. These changes include:

- self-employment to employment;
- individual to team working;
- self-management to external management;
- changes to pay;
- change of supervisor;
- changes in referral protocols;
- returns required;
- protocols and guidelines imposed;
- audit and evaluation;
- evidence-based practice;
- Agenda for Change job matching.

From the introduction of primary care commissioning, many counsellors have worked not knowing whether they had a contract, whether it would continue, whether their job would continue, whether their hours would increase or decrease, what their pay would be and whether they would have to change their supervisor. In addition there was, and still is, a major issue of who holds the power. Can counsellors be trusted to manage their own services, based in primary care, or should clinical psychologists in secondary care manage them? Throughout this they have managed to continue their client work and contain their clients' anxiety as well as their own. This is rarely recognised and appreciated and all the counsellors who have survived this deserve heartfelt congratulations and respect.

The NHS is again in the midst of another major change, with new proposals to reduce the number of PCTs – possibly to 150 from 302. This is as a result of *Commissioning a Patient-Led NHS* (Department of Health, 2005). The document initially looked to PCTs as commissioners and not providers of services. This would have a major impact on PCT-employed counsellors. Subsequently, there has been a shift away from this, which indicates that existing employed staff may well continue as they are. However, it is now extremely unlikely that a PCT yet to decide how to manage its primary care counselling provision would look to employing staff. The restructuring of PCTs could also mean more management change and the possibility of different employers.

Regulation

Not only have primary care counsellors struggled as they fought to establish themselves as a profession in primary care, they have also had the issue of regulation to contend with. Counselling and psychotherapy are not statutorily regulated professions; anyone can call himself or herself a counsellor and there are no nationally agreed standards as to what the training of a counsellor and psychotherapist should be. BACP accreditation and UKCP registration are the professions self-regulatory processes, but there are many who have not chosen to be bound by them.

There are a number of counsellors who passionately oppose regulation, and the need by standard setters to quantify the 'science' of counselling. Firmly held beliefs of counselling as an art, which is dependent on the interaction between two individuals alone, find the new structures problematic to say the least.

I would say that there are many more who would welcome regulation and standard setting as a way of making the profession safer for the public and as a badge of recognition. The underlying principle has to be that counselling is not just 'tea and sympathy' but is an intervention that can do both good or harm. That said, a safety net of standards in terms of training and practice provides a container that enables the counsellor to work effectively and the clients to know they are in safe hands.

The regulation debate continues, with strong indications from government that the Health Professions Council is the regulator of choice. However, there are other voices within the talking therapies professions who prefer the establishment of a Mental Health Council.

Context/Container

When we look at the context within which the counsellor has to work, Marilyn Pietroni and Alison Vaspe (2000) remind us that 'Donald Schon stresses the necessity of linking the elegant "high ground" of intellectual understanding with the murky "swamp" of everyday practice'. In this swamp we should reflect on the place of the GP surgery in society today. We have seen the church, education and social services devalued in the eyes of the public and with the Dr Harold Shipman case this has happened with doctors as well.

One of the most important roles provided by the counsellor is that of 'container'. Counsellors are able to contain fear around mental health issues, the anxieties of patients and staff. They can offer a normalising and acceptance of the human condition, which contains the individual's conscious and unconscious fears. This can be facilitated by the counsellor's understanding of unconscious processes that take place within the setting of the GP surgery. Awareness of the alliances that ebb and flow, the underlying anxieties that result in individuals taking rigid positions and the concomitant acting out that takes place gives the counsellor a privileged perspective. Utilising that perspective effectively requires a subtle skill, which can only be brought into play when the counsellor is viewed as a trusted member of the primary health care team.

In all areas, there is a much more informed and demanding public, who have instant access to information on the internet. This is juxtaposed with a dependence on the GP to 'cure' and again this can be in opposition to the work of the counsellor, which can be to 'contain'.

There is also relevance that though there are not a dominant number of male GPs, there can be at senior partner level. This can result in gender and power issues when it comes to recognition and respect of the work of the counsellor. This is particularly relevant when we bear in mind that, in 1999, 87 per cent of counsellors were white and female, with an average age of 48.1 years (Burton et al., 2001). Anecdotally it would seem that more men are working as counsellors today. However, it might be interesting to reflect on what might have been the consequences if the genders had been reversed and 87 per cent of counsellors were men.

The counsellor needs to introduce into this swamp a containing environment. One of the great benefits, in my view, of counsellors working in primary care is their focus on the importance of areas such as:

- being on time for appointments;
- ensuring there are no interruptions during the session;
- treating the client no differently in the NHS from the private or voluntary sectors;
- endeavouring to provide a suitable environment within the confines of the rooms available;

- being aware of the difficulties for some patients of being singled out as different and working to minimise these effects;
- understanding the acting out that may take place in terms of cancellations and non-attendance, but not allowing themselves to be exploited;
- the conscious and unconscious processes taking place.

Counsellors, operating from a position of positive regard, aim to provide a theoretical space that can enable the client to gain understanding, meaning and resolution of their problems. This is developed by Anna Bravesmith (1999), who states:

> in brief work in the GP surgery, I am relating to the patient as both myself and as a representative and part of the matrix, which consists of the group of workers in the surgery. The matrix continues to be available to the patients after our brief work is finished and I think the patient internalises the matrix, and the setting too, as a good object.

Resistance/Defences

Counsellors have had to contend with a continual questioning of the efficacy of their work not only with the NHS but also within the media. Part of this is lack of knowledge as to what counselling actually is. Jane Keithley says: 'we would suggest that many remain unsure of what counselling actually is. They still wonder what goes on in the counsellor's room, in those 50-minute or hour-long sessions. What is it that distinguishes a "talking therapy" from talking?' (Bond et al., 2002). It is interesting to speculate as to the fantasies that are prevalent concerning counselling, and people can be very threatened by it. Is this because of lack of knowledge, or fear of control of minds, or do counsellors challenge the rigid, fixed views held by many in our acceptance of difference?

We can be said to be in a position of lack of clarity as to what counselling is and how it works. Working in the NHS compounds this, as 'evidence-based practice' is the name of the game. This means that there has to be scientific evidence that the treatment being offered is proven to work.

The gold standard measurement is a randomised control trial, and, finally, the results of the 'Randomised controlled trial of non-directive counselling, cognitive-behaviour therapy, and usual general practitioner care for patients with depression' (Bower et al., 2000) were published. This concluded that employing practice-based counsellors or cognitive-based therapists might achieve a faster resolution of symptoms in patients with moderately severe depression. Despite some positive evidence, very much corroborated by CORE (described below), the attacks continue and have to be continually challenged, which can be very wearing for all concerned and undermining for the individual counsellor.

The most effective tool to measure clinical outcomes of a counselling intervention is CORE (Clinical Outcomes for Routine Evaluation; see www.coreims.co.uk), which is described by John Mellor-Clark (2004). However, here we encounter counsellor resistance. There is understandable fear at having one's performance measured and there can be all manner of reasons given as to why this is not a good idea. However, results obtained are extremely favourable and demonstrate the effectiveness of a counselling intervention.

So while we have to look at the resistances to counselling within the NHS and the media, we also have to consider counsellors' resistance to using an evaluation tool that could demonstrate how well they work. It is possible to conjecture that the primary care counselling profession feels attacked, backed into a corner and damned if it will go on proving that what it knows works – really does.

Counsellors are sometimes perceived as 'difficult' within primary health care teams because there is a lack of understanding about the boundaries of confidentiality. Counsellors came to the

NHS with very strong beliefs in the importance of confidentiality and a client-centred approach. This was on occasion somewhat challenging for other primary care health professionals, who were used to a very different culture of shared information. Effective communication as to why the counsellor's approach seemed different resulted in better understanding. Unfortunately, some counsellors became defensive and used 'confidentiality' to resist integration within the team.

There is a danger that this pressure can result in a defensive, powerless counsellor. The reaction to that can be anger, passive aggression or retreat into non-cooperation. The difficulty too is that the counsellor is isolated in his or her surgery and if not part of a counselling service has nowhere but supervision and perhaps his or her own therapy to take it.

Reflection

Attempting to pull together the themes of this chapter, and looking at the processes at play, I would now like to look at:

- What role the primary care counsellor is fulfilling in the surgery.
- What issues there are around belonging or otherwise to the primary health care team.
- How supervision affects the primary care counsellor.
- The consequence of different cultures meeting.
- Unacknowledged issues of omnipotence and arrogance.
- How training provision has enabled the development of the primary care counsellor.

Sher and Wiener (1998, p. 5) differentiate between maternal and paternal roles as follows: 'The demand is for the *maternal* giving of counselling rather than for the *paternal* authority of medicine, since notions of authority, leadership and power are often seen to form no part of the counsellor's role.' This description reflects a conflict within counsellors themselves. To survive in today's NHS they need to have authority, leadership and power, yet that does not sit comfortably with a 'maternal' role. The counsellor who is in conflict with himself or herself may become disempowered when in conflict with those in authority, whether in the surgery or the PCT.

Primary care counsellors have traditionally been individual workers. They are more often than not trained for private practice. The closest team working approaches may be in group supervision. This is compounded by often working on one's own in the surgery. In addition, counsellors are used to working in a dyad. Now they are also expected to be part of a team of counsellors and to think in terms of their colleagues as well as themselves.

Another interesting change brought about by the introduction of primary care counselling is described by Keithley: 'Counselling, like social work before it, also introduces the important concept of supervision, a notion previously rather alien to medicine' (Bond et al., 2002, p. 35). This is a challenge to the omnipotence of other health professionals. Counsellors believe that supervision is essential to their practice. This is not just in terms of hierarchical, educative supervision; even the most experienced practitioners will still have blind spots and will experience each of their clients as unique. Supervision is not the norm within the medical profession, though there is now an increase in a mentoring role for colleagues (as the chapter on mentoring included in this book shows). It could be said that: 'The presence of a counsellor in the practice offers the opportunity to expand the psychological resources of the practice as a whole and represents an attempt to keep psyche and soma connected at all levels, and thus to mend the ruptures that have existed for so many years' (Sher and Wiener, 1998, p. 17).

Supervision is also an opportunity for counsellors to explore the transference and counter-transference that is taking place. This is in the context of both client work and the individuals in the primary health care team. In addition, there will be transference to the organisational culture and the danger of splitting between good and bad objects: the good PCT, the bad psychology service. Our training enables us to be open to such processes and it is to be hoped that gaining understanding as to what is being acted out by those around us and by ourselves will make us more effective both in our work with our clients and in our dealings with the system within which we choose to work.

As these two cultures met there needs to be awareness of what may be taking place, Jan Wiener (1996, p. 29) describes it thus: 'The old Cartesian split between mind and body has had an undermining effect on the entire field of mental health. Doctors can overvalue the "objective" body, neglecting patients' subjective experience of their bodies; counsellors and psychotherapists are often tempted to ignore or interpret away patients' actual medical symptoms.' Andrew Elder (1996) reinforces this: 'The mind – in general practice, just like the mind in life – is inseparable from the body and the two are frequently muddled up, the mind speaking for the body at one moment and the body speaking for the mind at others.'

The danger of thinking with a singular view – it is either the mind or the body – rather than it is both, is one that has to be in the awareness of both medical and counselling practitioners. There is a danger of arrogance when one dismisses the other, and while it may seem obvious to us on the printed page, I would suggest that many counselling practitioners can go through an omnipotent phase of thinking that counselling can be used to cure all ills.

It is also interesting to reflect whether counselling in primary care developed as a way to deal with the stigma of a 'psychiatric referral'. Is a referral to counselling a much more acceptable intervention for mental distress? The primary care counsellor is part of a normalising culture within primary care. Referral criteria for primary care counsellors are often characterised in terms of life crises as opposed to medical labels. However, again there is a danger of omnipotence, that counselling can be used to treat every mental illness, and that is palpably not the case.

It could be said that primary care counsellors have had to fight long and hard to establish themselves as firmly as they have within the NHS. It is interesting that the battle has been on many fronts. There is the conflict between medical and holistic approaches, between commissioners and practitioners, between managers and staff and between counsellors and other talking therapy professionals. Mary Burton describes this thus:

> In the mental health field, it has sadly become commonplace to hear one profession attacking another as lacking the clinical skills to deal with the patients referred to them. As long as these rivalries are understood as the social defences they are, we do not fall into the trap of holding our colleagues in contempt. (Burton, 1998, p. 13)

Training

The remit of this book is to look at training standards. This chapter on the history of primary care counselling provides a backcloth to the rest of the book. Training provision since the inception of primary care counselling has, to say the least, been variable and patchy. The glory years of specialist primary care counselling courses (as described in much greater detail in Penny Henderson's chapter) were the six MAs in primary care counselling set up with a number of universities, including Sussex, Bristol, Stratchclyde and Salford under the sponsorship and guidance of the Counselling in Primary Care Trust under the directorship of Dr Graham Curtis Jenkins. Dr Curtis-Jenkins recently commented that those who pursued these MAs are now in senior management positions within the primary care counselling world – a great success story. This success fell down somewhat when they became free standing without sponsorship, underlining my earlier point about the need for good grant funding.

We are at a watershed in primary care counselling, with the sort of acceptance that we have never achieved before. To match this we urgently need quality provision of training for the specialist primary care counsellor. The paramount necessity is for the employer (the NHS) to work with the training institutions to ensure that counsellors are trained to be fit for the purpose. Statutory regulation may be the lever that forces this to happen, which would be regrettable. It is the hope of all those involved in the production of this book that it will itself be part of this process, will raise understanding and will result in effective links between the trainers and the employers.

In conclusion, it is a valid truth that there is more work to be done in the field of mental health than can be done by any single profession. It is to be hoped that the growth of primary care counselling will be a welcome addition to the resources required and that the place of the primary care counsellor will be firmly established and valued in the NHS.

I hope that this chapter may promote a greater level of understanding of the processes that underlie the development of primary care counselling in the NHS. In turn, this may give us a slightly more informed base from which to continue our development in the future.

Notes

1 http://www.dh.gov.uk/PolicyAndGuidance/HumanResourcesAndTraining/ModernisingPay/AgendaForChange/fs/en

References

Addington-Hall, J., Brenneman, D., Freeling, P. and Sibbald, B. (1993) Counsellors in English and Welsh practices, their nature and distribution. *British Medical Journal*, 306, 29–33.

Barr, J. and Marsh, G. N. (1975) Marriage guidance counselling in a group practice. *Journal of the Royal College of General Practitioners*, 25, 73–5.

Bond, T., Keithley, J. and Marsh, G. (2002) *Counselling in Primary Care*, 2nd edn. Oxford: Oxford University Press.

Bor, R. and McCann, D. (1999) *The Practice of Counselling in Primary Care*. London: Sage.

Bower, P., Byford, S., Gabbay, M., King, M., Lloyd, M., Sibbald, B. and Ward, E. (2000) Randomised controlled trial of non-directive counselling, cognitive-behaviour therapy and usual general practitioner care for patients with depression. *British Medical Journal*, 321.

Bravesmith, A. (ed.) (1999) *The Matrix at Work: A Post-Jungian Approach to General Practice Counselling*. London: Routledge.

Burton, M. (1998) *Psychotherapy, Counselling and Primary Mental Health Care*. Chichester, Wiley.

Burton, M., Mellor-Clark, J. and Simms-Ellis, R. (2001) *National Survey of Counsellors Working in Primary Care: Evidence for Growing Professionalisation?* London: Royal College of General Practitioners, Occasional Paper 79.

Department of Health (1998) *Primary Care Groups: Delivering the Agenda*. Health Service Circular 1998/28. London: HMSO.

Department of Health (1999) *National Service Framework for Mental Health*. London: HMSO.

Department of Health (2001) *Treatment Choice in Psychological Therapies and Counselling: Evidence Based Clinical Practice Guideline*. London: HMSO.

Department of Health (2005) *Commissioning a Patient-led NHS*. London: HMSO.

Elder, A. (1996) Primary care and psychotherapy. Paper in Conference Proceedings: *Future Directions of Psychotherapy in the NHS: Adaption or Extinction, 10*, p. 60.

Hinshelwood, R. (1996) Psychiatry and Psychotherapy. *Psychoanalytic Psychotherapy*, 10(suppl.), 5–10.

Lees, J. (1999) Clinical counselling in primary care. In A. Bravesmith (ed.), *The Matrix at Work: A Post-Jungian Approach to General Practice Counselling*. London: Routledge.

Mellor-Clark, J. (2004) A review of the evolution of research evidence and activity for NHS primary care counselling. *Psychodynamic Practice*, 10(3), 373–93.

Mental Health National Service Framework and the NHS Plan, Workforce Planning, Education and Training, Underpinning Programme (2001) *Adult Mental Health Services: Final Report by the Workforce Action Team, Special Report*, Appendix C, p. 27 (available at www.doh.gov.uk/nsf/mentalhealth.htm).

Pietroni, M. and Vaspe, A. (2000) *Understanding Counselling in Primary Care: Voices from the Inner City*. Edinburgh: Churchill Livingstone.

Sher, M. and Wiener, J. (1998) *Counselling and Psychotherapy in Primary Health Care: A Psychodynamic Approach*. London: Macmillan Press.

Wiener, J. (1996) Looking out and looking in: some reflections on 'body talk' in the consulting room. *Journal of Analytical Psychology*, 39, 3.

CHAPTER TWO

Why Go to All This Trouble?

Douglas Hooper and Philippa Weitz

IN Chapter One of this book Joan Foster has outlined the recent history of the rise and rise of counselling in primary care mental health provision. There are at least the following professional practitioners involved in mental health services directly or indirectly with general practitioner and their patients:

- counsellor;
- psychiatrist;
- community psychiatric nurse;
- clinical psychologist;
- nurse behaviour therapist;
- general practitioner.

In addition there are other practitioners in the wings of secondary care who may be involved, but are less easily available. All of these practitioners will have gone through a basic and then further training to equip them for their work, although that may often be generic rather than specific to the primary care setting. The argument in this book and in this chapter is that to deliver an effective counselling and psychotherapeutic service directly and *in situ* to patients in their community setting needs 'situation-specific' forms of training and education, which are unlikely to have been covered in their earlier experience. Later chapters will spell out in detail the areas that we believe should be the essential learning for primary care practice, but the question remains as to why it should be done in the first place. Is not the generic training that counsellors receive broadly adequate in meeting the mental health problems of the general practice clientele, regardless of the setting and the presentation of the problems? If the counsellor is competently trained to, say, the standard required for accreditation by the British Association of Counselling and Psychotherapy (BACP), is that not enough? This, after all, purports to certify that the person is effectively trained for professional practice as a counsellor, following evaluation of both the training and the practice he or she has undertaken and the decision that this will be acceptable to any agency employing the person.

Joan Foster tells us that this was, indeed, enough in the earlier period of counselling practice in primary care. In fact the early counsellors were not even trained to the BACP standards because they were very frequently counsellors from the then Marriage Guidance Council seconded to work in the general practice setting. At that stage the training of these counsellors was certainly up to the level of accredited counsellors – however experienced they might have been.

The previous chapter points out for us that the work of Enid and Michael Balint was formative in addressing the psychological issues of primary care medical practice, but in fact it was about two decades before the search for a counselling presence in the surgery began in earnest. It is difficult to account for this hiatus, although Joan Foster thinks it is due to societal changes that were also taking place. It is not unreasonable to suppose that one major factor was the increasing knowledge and sophistication of the patients themselves about the availability of counsellors and counselling. This may have translated into requests by patients to the GP for counselling rather than drugs for their treatment. Certainly, later studies have demonstrated how popular counselling became for patients in those practices where it was available.

Next we have to consider the dramatic rise in the number of people emerging from counsellor training in the 1980s and 1990s, many of whom were looking for areas of practice, which included primary health care. It seems that many GP practices were quite willing to give a counsellor houseroom, apart from the contracted counsellors who were provided by a local Relate centre. The mushrooming training programmes often required student counsellors to find placements for themselves and primary care was a home frequently used for this purpose – particularly as the counsellors almost always offered their services for free! Then, when they were qualified at the basic level, they might be able to find a practice 'home' in the same surgery. In other words, it looked, for a time, as if there was a curious synergy between the output of counsellors and the GPs' increasing recognition that they could play a useful if modest part in the delivery of health care. Counsellors could deal with social and emotional problems at the therapeutic coalface and without the patient having to seek help by referral to a somewhat alien secondary care system.

This haphazard marriage between a GP and a counsellor meant that the service delivered was going to be of a very variable quality indeed, since most GPs would have no idea about the basic qualifications of a particular counsellor. Further, the counsellors might make a somewhat breathless assumption that 'counselling is counselling is counselling' and that they could bend their skills to suit the needs of the patient. This was a strange assumption because it was not one that almost all the other primary health care practitioners would make. Certainly the nurse and doctors would generally speaking have had some additional training for their professional practice in the specific milieu of the general practice.

What is the actual scope for the practice of psychological therapies in this setting? We can put together some simple statistics that will illustrate the apparent need in an average practice for the sort of service that a counsellor/psychological therapist can deliver.

Supply and Demand

Let us look at some demographic data.

- One in every three or four patients (i.e. 25–30 per cent) who attends a doctor's appointment is in need of some mental health support (Layard, 2004). In the majority of instances, up to 90 per cent (Department of Health, 1999), this support will never need to be psychiatric specialist care, but will be general counselling/psychological support within the primary care system. If we take seven minutes as the average appointment with the general practitioner, he or she will see two or three patients per hour with a mental health need. Over an eight-hour day for one GP that might mean 16 patients attending with a mental health need. Over a five-day week that total rises to 80 consultations for every GP in the country.
- There are 8,000 doctors' surgeries in the UK housing approximately 35,000 doctors, with an approximate list of 2,000 each – that brings us to our total population.
- That is 2,800,000 patients needing some mental health support at any one time as a result of a week's appointments, and of course people don't go to the doctor every week so the number is likely to be higher.
- Put another way, one-third of our GPs are seeing, at any one time in the working day, someone with a mental health need.

Case Study of Patients and Clients Using the Above Figures

The fictional Beeches Surgery in London has five GPs, and a full-time (37 hours) and a part-time (20 hours) counsellor, i.e. 57 counselling hours including all paperwork and meetings. So perhaps 50 clinical hours are available, which is equal to 50 client hours, although we would question the ethics of such a heavy client load.

Five GPs means 400 patients attending with a wide range of mental health needs. Of these patients, 10 per cent (40 people) are likely to be referred on to specialist psychiatric care, and 40 per cent (160 people) never get diagnosed because they present with somatic problems. The picture then looks like this:

Referred to specialist services	40 patients (10%)
Lack of diagnosis	160 patients (40%)
Prescribed only anti-depressants (counselling apparently not needed)	80 patients (20%)
Those prescribed counselling (not including any of those in the other percentages who might also benefit)	120 patients (30%)

So at the end of this first week 50 patients might be referred to the counsellor in the practice, 70 patients go on a waiting list, or possibly might get referred on to another counselling agency (who pays for this counselling?).

Using figures such as these we can draw conclusions nationally about supply and demand. Let's stick to the lower figure of 30 per cent benefiting from counselling.

We have 700,000 – that is, 25 per cent of 2,800,000 (one in four patients needing mental health support at any time) – patients needing some counselling at any one time. Let us say they all get referred to the practice counsellor. That means the equivalent of 700,000 counselling hours, and the patient/client usually has six sessions, so some additional multiplication is necessary, but already the magnitude of the situation is clear. Disregarding any note writing and meeting time, with counsellors working a 7.5-hour day (not taking into account that this would be an impossibility for most counsellors), we need a minimum of 112,000 counsellors to fulfil supply and demand, in 8,000 general practices. That is the equivalent of 14 counsellors per general practice. In fact, our best guess is that we believe there may be around 3,000 counsellors working in primary care, many of whom have not received the specialist training required.

The picture we have painted here is astonishing. Although the gross figures presented above must be subject to qualification, the demand appears to be far greater than the present supply.

Current Training Provision

The best available data come from the research carried out by Penny Henderson for the Counselling and Psychotherapy Forum in Primary Care (Henderson, 2000), which showed that there are around nine specialist primary care courses leading to qualification as a primary care counsellor. There may also be another ten courses (such as one at the Tavistock Institute) providing a specialist 'bolt-on' certificate that aims to bring someone with a generalist training up to standard in primary care counselling.

So a generous estimate would be that there may be 19 such courses at any one time in the country, training probably a maximum of 15 students each. Thus there may a maximum of 285 primary care counsellors qualifying as a QCA Level 4 practitioner, the practitioner entry level to the profession, in any one year – well below what appears to be needed.

The point of these figures is to demonstrate that not only do we have a current counselling workforce that is largely unqualified for the special needs of primary care, but we are also not providing enough specialist training. Yet so often the courses collapse because of lack of take-up. So what is the problem? Well, of course, it is money.

The courses exist, but currently who pays for both the student fees and the courses? The student. Work by ENTO commissioned by the government has resulted in a suite of QCA qualifications for counselling, which should ensure that once they have the imprimatur of a QCA approved awarding body, funding follows. This is clearly one of the routes along which specialist counselling training must go in order to gain funding, and hence students.

All of this needs also to take account of the average age of counsellors currently working in primary care, which is probably between 45 and 60; in other words, generally at the older end of the workforce. The economics of the situation tell us we need to be training many new counsellors now to replace those who will retire in the not too distant future in order simply to maintain the workforce, let alone to expand it. In addition, the stepped care approaches and commitments to providing mental health care *for all* ensures that primary care counsellors will have an important role to play in the rolling out of these exciting and well overdue plans (Department of Health, 2004).

On the basis of this discussion it certainly appears that there is a good case for 'going to all this trouble' in terms of the mental health needs of general practice patients, despite the fact that general practitioners will also make use of mental practitioners other than counsellors.

What About the Patients?

There is plenty of evidence now that patients often request to 'see a counsellor' rather than take a prescribed drug for moderate depression or anxiety, and that, broadly speaking, they are satisfied or very satisfied with the counselling intervention. Note that this observation is different from the use of some evaluative instrument, which is directed at, for example, symptom removal or alleviation. GPs too, are generally very favourable to the work of counsellors in their practice. The popularity of counsellors is clear in the degree to which practices now employ counsellors. In a recent study of primary health care in the London area three-quarters of the practices had the services of a counsellor – yet a quarter of these same practices also reported that patients often had a long wait to see the counsellor (Adams et al., 2003).

Does a well trained counsellor of the kind we are proposing here provide a better service to patients than one who has not received any training or a basic qualification? At present we have no definitive answer to that particular question – the research waits to be done – but plenty of anecdotal evidence points to that being the case. This is also confirmed by these writers' experience of evaluating students on the specialist courses described later in this book.

Unfortunately some of the critical research into the efficacy of counselling in primary care has used counsellors who were clearly less than well trained, and has sometimes called the practitioners under study 'counsellors' when they were other health professionals such as nurses. Much of this research has been subject to a scholarly critique by Hemmings. He concludes his paper by writing: '[the research] has largely evaluated the practice of mental health practitioners who have used psychological interventions as part of their work, but rarely evaluated practitioners who have completed an accreditable training' (Hemmings, 1999, p. 29). It must surely be the case that a patient being counselled by a competent counsellor (as defined in this book) is going to receive a far better professional deal than one not so trained because of the coverage in professional practice that such a training will provide.

The Practitioner

We will finally focus on the advantages to counsellors themselves of spending their time, energy and money on achieving a specialist standard of practice.

Of great importance is the recognition of counsellors by the National Health Service in the staff and grading structures. This is dealt with in detail elsewhere in this book, but it means that there will be an expectancy on the part of employers that the standards now agreed will apply to new would-be practitioners. At present the standards do not closely specify the detailed specialist preparation required, but it is clear that they are implied.

This is the mirror image of another of the advantages of the specialist training for counsellors. When they have completed further training primary care counsellors are much more confident in their own practice and in their relationships with their health care colleagues. This has already been demonstrated in Joan Foster's chapter on history: the original MA courses in primary care counsellors have left us with a very skilled group of people now in high-ranking positions in primary care counselling. These courses may have been before their time and have left something of a vacuum but they may provide us with a vision for the future of primary care counselling training.

The advanced training that we propose here results in practitioners being both knowledgeable and confident. It will have made them examine carefully the counselling role and its relationship to other professionals. They will have become aware and knowledgeable about the different universes of health discourse that are used – particularly by doctors and nurses. In other words they will be much more fit to practise the 'First Class Service' propounded for the NHS (Department of Health, 1998).

Next there is the advantage of equipping practitioners with the knowledge and skills not only to advance their own practice through CPD schemes, but also to be able to understand and evaluate research and other new knowledge in the psychological therapies in primary care. Well trained counsellors do not necessarily have to undertake research themselves, but they need to be aware of the research and development in the field. Where necessary they should also be able to cooperate with others in the team who do undertake some practice research. One of the noteworthy elements in the earlier MA training programmes funded by the Counselling in Primary Care Trust was the requirement that graduates should have undertaken a small study on their own.

The last advantage to practitioners is that they are able to contribute to the broader issues of complex mental health issues in their employment practices because they are confident about their own skills repertoire. The days when the 'counsellor' appeared, did the work and disappeared without sharing ideas and concerns with other people should be over. In addition, the competent counsellor is then in a position both to supervise others and perhaps – if necessary – to mentor the work of other professionals who may be encouraged to use more complex counselling skills in their own practice.

Conclusion

In this short compass we have tried to demonstrate how the need for the competent counsellor is now paramount in primary health care. The role has grown and matured over the past decade and is now fully recognised in the manpower planning of the NHS. In this chapter we have not tried to encompass discussion about the role of counsellors compared with other mental health practitioners noted at the beginning but simply put the case for answering the question posed by the chapter in a firm and resounding way. This paves the way for the remaining chapters to describe in detail how the 'bother' can be competently exercised.

References

Adams, B., Dolley, T. and Hampton, J. (2003) Ideal and actual choices for mental health problems in primary care. *Counselling Psychology Review*, 18, 20–33.

Department of Health (1998) *A First Class Service: Quality in the NHS* (HSC1998/113). London: HMSO.

Department of Health (1999) *National Service Framework for Mental Health*. London: HMSO.

Department of Health (2004) *Organising and Delivering Psychological Therapies*. London: HMSO.

Hemmings, A. (1999) *A Systematic Review of Brief Psychological Therapies in Primary Health Care*. Staines: Counselling in Primary Care Trust.

Henderson, P. (2000) *A Study of Training Provision in Primary Healthcare Counselling in the UK*. Brighton: Counselling and Psychotherapy Forum in Primary Care.

Layard, Lord R. (2004) *Mental Health: Britain's Biggest Social Problem?* (available from www.strategy.gov.uk/downloads/files/mh_layard. pdf).

CHAPTER THREE

The Link between Training and Good Practice and the Implementation of Training Standards

What Does This Mean for Employers?

Joan Foster and Philippa Weitz

The Antecedents to the Current Problem

GIVEN that in 2000 there were fewer than ten primary care counselling courses it is highly unlikely that anything but a very small minority of counsellors will have received appropriate training for the job. Existing practitioners have learnt 'on the job', which is not the ideal way to ensure best practice.

Sadly, informal stories gleaned from the press, friends and clients tell us that appropriate care of our clients is still not always happening. As professionals, *we have a public duty to ensure that training is appropriate for practice and available to the number of students needing to train.*

Society has seen fundamental and profound changes since the Second World War and of particular relevance to the development of counselling in primary care is the decline in voluntary work and the need for women to support themselves. The ethos of voluntary counselling agencies struggling to provide low-cost counselling continues to this day, and trainee counsellors often find placements in voluntary agencies. The availability of placements can be problematic with the continuing increase in the number of training courses for counsellors. The expectation of counsellors training today is that they will be able to earn money from their work and so there is a danger that voluntary agencies will end up being staffed by students.

There is a challenge to many helping professions, whereby there may be a perception that because there is a vocational aspect to the work, pay should not be important. Our personal view is that the work counsellors do is highly skilled and emotionally demanding and the counsellors should be rewarded accordingly. However, for many there could be a cultural heritage of work in the voluntary sector, which may have hindered their ability to negotiate adequate pay and conditions.

The Vision: Providing Employers with a Framework of Competence and Knowledge for Counselling in Primary Care

When the Counselling and Psychotherapy Forum for Primary Care was set up in 1999 it had a clear vision, in the face of all these difficulties, of what was needed to train counsellors to work in GP practices. Lead professional bodies (see Appendix 1 for the list of participants) came together and were able to identify with relative ease the areas of expertise required of primary care counsellors and how these could be addressed in their training.

Regrettably it then became a case of one step forward and two steps back. The Forum was challenged in how to transmit its thinking to the training community, the NHS, the awarding bodies and other professional bodies.

Although there was some success in involving ENTO[1] and QCA, the response from training bodies was more limited. At a presentation to a number of training bodies, the proposals were not viewed (by the training institutions) as relevant to the training currently provided. We were very surprised at some of this feedback: if we transported this to any other field of education, training providers would surely organise their training around established and recognised guidelines; otherwise they would not have students. This is a reflection of the lack of defined standards, because counselling and psychotherapy are not statutorily regulated. It is therefore apparent that we need to ensure that students are aware of these standards so that they can select their course appropriately.

Turning to those who are already trained, from meetings with many counsellors around the country, it would appear that the majority are not trained for purpose to work in the NHS, although we are not aware of research in this area to substantiate this view. Does counselling training adequately prepare counsellors to work within the NHS – a medical system? We mean not that counsellors should be medically trained, but that they should be trained to work as part of a team in a large organisation, should be accountable and should be able to provide counselling that complements existing services within the NHS. This need has been identified as follows:

> Our own experience as practitioners, supervisors and trainers has taught us that to seek to develop counselling skills without an understanding of the complex dynamics of health care teams and management skills is potentially self-defeating and could even inadvertently put the counsellor on a collision course with whom he or she most closely works. (Bor and McCann, 1999)

Another key issue with training is the cost. The vast majority of counsellors have to pay large fees for their training and personal therapy, which can exclude those not able to afford such high sums. The work members of the Forum have recently done with the QCA in reviewing the National Vocational Qualification's (NVQ's) suite of counselling qualifications opens the door potentially to funding. If a course has the endorsement of a QCA awarding body then it will receive government funding, which will reduce the cost to the student. Currently these NVQs have been set from Level 1 through to Level 8 (PhD level) with counselling skills being on Level 3 and practitioner entry level to the profession being set at Level 4. For the moment there are no specialist suites available for primary care counsellors, but we hope this will follow. All this is positive prior to the anticipated arrival of statutory regulation, which may take place in 2008, and this work may even have some influence on how regulation is implemented.

The Politics of the NHS

We can never, in any role in the NHS, escape the rapidly changing politics. We are in a time of change and evolution in the NHS. Within mental health the current plans in *Organising and Developing Psychological Therapies* (Department of Health, 2004) and Lord Layard's report (Layard, 2004) are encouraging in so far as they encourage a proper integrated mental health service available to all, but the reality is that this is still undergoing change, and we all know how uncomfortable change is. Whatever the status of these changes, the general public, and we on their behalf, expect our counsellors to be highly trained for work in the NHS in the twenty-first century so that they can take their place as equal and valued members of the primary care team providing for the integrated health care of the client and patient.

What Changes Are There in the Clinical Setting?

If the current thinking is implemented then primary care counsellors will take their place as part of a stepped care approach in which the principle is that the service user enters at a level of therapeutic intervention at the lowest intensity and cost appropriate for the individual's symptoms, only progressing to a 'higher' intensity if this is not effective. Primary care counselling will take its place within this approach, but possibly with a dictat from the Department of Health to administer cognitive-behavioural therapy. This has its problems, because setting up a one-size-fits-all therapeutic intervention does not reflect the realities of the needs of the individual, which are infinitely variable.

We continue to think that training organisations have not fully got to grips with the needs of the NHS as an employer. Equally, NHS employers are not fully aware of:

1 How qualified some primary care counsellors are.
2 What qualifications and competences they need in order to provide quality care in the twenty-first century NHS.

We believe that the Minimum Training Standards for Primary Care Counselling (Appendix 2) and the Person Specification Criteria (Appendix 3) as set out and published by the Forum provide the framework and standard of competence required. We are unclear why training organisations have been so reluctant to implement them.

The Training Organisations

This is still a very unsure world where the viability of a course is critical. We therefore have courses chasing any number of students so that the course and college will have a secure future. This does not, however, ensure the quality of courses. Penny Henderson's (2000) mapping exercise of primary care counselling courses is now six years old and, while a lot has changed, courses suitable for a budding primary care counsellor are in short supply, and subject to being axed because of lack of funding. Additionally it is of interest, that, of the six MAs in primary care counselling, only a few have survived.

It has been a relief to know that ENTO/QCA has put into place criteria that the whole industry agrees on, from the professional membership organisation to the awarding bodies. This provides trainers, for the first time, with national criteria to work to; those who are serious about statutory regulation will welcome these as a first step. There is one serious flaw, however: these criteria do not include degree courses, which come under a different umbrella, the Quality Assurance Agency, which has not yet been involved in discussions concerning levels and standards.

On a more positive note, the demographic data in Chapter Two show us that there will continue to be demand for well trained counsellors working in primary care. So the challenge is now set to training organisations to start providing courses, either as part of a first training or as a specialist bolt-on diploma for the primary care counsellor.

Minimum Standards of Training and Competence for Primary Care Counsellors, Counselling Trainees, Training Organisations and Employers

The work of the Counselling and Psychotherapy Forum for Primary Care has been to provide a framework to prepare counsellors adequately to work with the needs of today's and tomorrow's clients. Although the work is now a little dated, there is nothing that is more recent. Appendices 2 and 3 provide the full standards and criteria documents. Here is a summary:

- Initial generic counselling training, including 450 hours of core theoretical model(s) and skills training. This level of counselling training needs to be acceptable to the relevant professional bodies and will also lead to accreditation/registration with BACP/CPC.

Plus

- assessment (including mental health and risk management);
- ethical frameworks for professional practice;
- general legal issues;
- working with diversity;
- 40 hours minimum of *personal development* (this means individual personal therapy);
- 100 hours minimum of *managed and supervised clinical placement*.

The Forum considers two models of training particularly appropriate:

- A minimum of three years of generic counselling/psychotherapy training plus a minimum of one year post qualification for primary care counselling training. Or
- A four-year training, which includes all requirements. The final year would introduce a brief/focal model or demonstrate how the taught model is applied in a brief/focal way.

Primary care specific trainings need to be *context specific* and prepare trainees in *time limited work*.

In addition, primary care training courses need to include, or provide bolt-on modules for, the following:

- psychotropic drugs/medication;
- primary health care team relationships;
- NHS structure;
- assessment, particularly when working to a time limit;
- knowledge of mental health referral pathways and procedures;
- brief focused therapy methods.

We would also recommend in all training, and require for primary care training, input on:

- Interactive processes in families.
- Systemic theory.
- Audit and evaluation methodologies.
- Behavioural therapeutic approaches (these were not included in the original training specifications but the authors have added them because of the Department of Health's insistence on their effectiveness, and therefore in order to be more employable it will be important for counsellors to have experience of cognitive-behavioural therapy).
- Supervision. Supervision plays a key role and *must* be relevant to primary care. The training supervisor needs to have a specific knowledge or experience of primary care and of brief focused therapy, with a suggested ratio of one hour of supervision to six clinical hours.
- Mentoring (covered more fully in a later chapter). Placements are made only under the guidance of a mentor, and mentoring should be seen as distinct from supervision.
- Quality assurance. Audit, evaluation and research-based practice.

Training Placements

Although there is a chapter dedicated to placements and mentoring, we believe that they require far higher quality control and emphasis than is currently the case, and we have added our own section to this chapter to highlight this point. For a more detailed discussion please see Chapter Ten.

What Changes Are There in Placement Processes?

Sadly, there are not enough. Ideally the placement system should be a contractual partnership between the training organisation and the employing organisation, which provides the training placement scheme. All too often students still have to find their own placements, and so often are receiving inappropriate client referrals. This, of course, puts both patients and clients at risk.

The procedures for training placements for student counsellors are of relevance when we are exploring the history of the development of primary care counselling. Traditionally, the culture has been that student counsellors were required to obtain their own placements, often supplied with a list from the training organisation. One of the standard suggestions was to ring their local GP and ask if they could work for free in the surgery to gain the required clinical hours of experience. This approach generates some interesting dynamics:

- Will the student be trained to work to a time limit or be offering open-ended counselling?
- The student will most probably have no training in assessment and risk assessment.
- The GPs will not be given referral guidelines as to appropriate referrals for the student.
- The student will have no preparation for working in an organisation such as the NHS.
- The student may not have any training in mental illnesses, medication and legal issues.
- The feedback structures among the GP, the supervisor and the training institution are rarely clear.
- The student may not have been CRB checked.

The unstated presumption is that counsellors can do no harm and therefore can safely work with any client group in any circumstance. We would challenge this assumption in its entirety. The logical consequence of that is 'what is the need for training at all, if nothing can go wrong?' If we do not take ourselves seriously as a profession and arrange mentored placements for our students, our professional colleagues will not take us seriously. It has to be recognised that poorly delivered counselling can do harm and that counsellors working out of their depth can do harm. It is important to remember that we don't know what we don't know and unless our teachers, employers and colleagues tell us, we will never learn.

We should ask ourselves what other profession does not link training to the workplace. Leaving a student to find a placement as part of the 'process' of the training would seem to us to indicate a lack of responsibility on behalf of the training institution. It also results in an interesting dynamic as follows:

> In a Primary Care Trust, the local MIND service provides student placements. The PCT has a primary care counselling service, with a team of highly qualified counsellors. The perception of the PCT and GPs is that MIND is where more complex, longer-term clients are referred and the clients with mild to moderate problems are sent to the primary care counsellor. Understanding of the training needs of students could result in a change of commissioning so that the experienced counsellors could work with longer-term complex cases and the students could start with clients with less complex problems.

This lack of understanding of the level of training required to produce an appropriately qualified counsellor can result in PCTs thinking that the solution to their resource problems is to put in large numbers of student counsellors. The exact parallel would be a school of probationer teachers. The professional bodies have to take some responsibility for this misconception, recognising that not everyone can become a counsellor and that bad counselling is damaging. Everyone has to learn but within properly managed placement schemes, with input to the training organisation, a three-way contract and the power to stop poor performers.

Accreditation/Registration: What Does It All Mean?

Pity the poor PCT Mental Health Commissioner trying to write a service specification for a primary care counselling service. What level of training should be required? Until the professional bodies agree, no employer has much chance of understanding what is required. Is a counsellor straight out of college appropriate, is a counsellor accredited by a grandparenting route with little training appropriate? What does BACP Accreditation, CPC Registration or UKCP Registration mean?

To confuse the situation even more, where do National Vocational Qualifications (NVQs) sit? Some 51 per cent of counselling trainings are at diploma level. This is NVQ Level 4. The Health Professions Council normally, but not exclusively, looks to regulate degree-level professions (NVQ Level 6). The new Psychotherapeutic Counselling Section of UKCP has set its standards at degree level. UKCP Psychotherapy Trainings are at degree or masters level.

What does the primary care counsellor require? The Counselling and Psychotherapy Forum for Primary Care looked to a post-qualification one-year training for a primary care counsellor. It needs to be recognised that this post-qualification training would include critical areas such as risk assessment and working to a time limit, psychotropic medication and mental illnesses. A key concern is that many trainings offer at the most a short module in working to a time limit and that the understanding of the demands of this are often not realised by the student.

Students are in a hurry and want to get out to earn money. Being told that a year's work post-qualification to consolidate their practice before moving into a workplace student placement on a one-year primary care counselling course is unlikely to be well received. We need to take seriously the theoretical underpinning of training to ensure standards are not sacrificed to expediency.

Where Are We Now?

There are some training sites around the country, but there are many who have yet to pick up the challenge of workplace placements. This, of course, is understandable because it is organisationally complex. However, our belief is that until we make this transition, we cannot truly consider ourselves a profession.

The question has to be: what is stopping this happening? It is of course more than the organisational complexities. The NHS is changing structurally at breakneck pace and for the poor training organisation it is too big a task to try to understand whom to contact to make this happen. The way forward is for formal links to be established by the managers of counselling services and the training organisations. This would be through the Network of Service Providers and CPC, BACP and UKCP. However, that is a great deal easier said than done! The service managers are battling for survival at the time of writing, and practice-based commissioning and the patient-led NHS changes are only beginning to be put in place.

A Success Story?

Unfortunately, not yet! There is a long way to go before we can consider the training needs of potential primary care counsellors as being met – the challenge is there for training providers to prepare well constructed focused training courses fit for the training of the primary care counsellor in the twenty-first century.

Note

1 ENTO is a privately run organisation committed to developing the competence of people who work with people through the use of National Occupational Standards (NOS) and other means where appropriate.

References

Bor, R. and McCann, D. (1999) *The Practice of Counselling in Primary Care*. London: Sage.

Counselling and Psychotherapy Forum for Primary Care (2001a) *Minimum Training Standards for Primary Care Counselling*. Brighton: Counselling and Psychotherapy Forum for Primary Care.

Counselling and Psychotherapy Forum for Primary Care (2001b) *Person Specification Criteria*. Brighton: Counselling and Psychotherapy Forum for Primary Care.

Department of Health (2004) *Organising and Delivering Psychological Therapies*. London: HMSO.

Henderson, P. (2000) *A Study of Training Provision in Primary Healthcare Counselling in the UK*. Brighton: Counselling and Psychotherapy Forum for Primary Care.

Layard, Lord R. (2004) *Mental Health: Britain's Biggest Social Problem?* (available from www.strategy.gov.uk/downloads/files/mh_layard. pdf).

Part II

Training Programmes – Institutional and Placement

CHAPTER FOUR

Fitness to Be Trained

The Selection of Trainees and Course Content: A Trainer's View

John Eatock

WHILE on my way to Edinburgh, at Preston station, on Tuesday 26 August 2003, I happened to pick up a copy of the *Guardian* to read on the train. I was very struck by an article on a book called 'Mike May's diary'. Three years ago Mike May's sight was partially restored by a pioneering transplant using stem cells. Neuroscientists were just releasing their analysis of the effects of the operation on his brain. So on that day the *Guardian* was publishing his account of seeing for the first time since he was three, and now he is aged 43. As you might imagine, the description of Mike's experience fascinated me on my journey. I was particularly intrigued as to how he had to learn to develop an ability to identify colour, shapes and even movements. Slowly but surely, over a period of years he has worked very hard on integrating his new-found vision into his other sensory perceptions. He found that his new ability to see often dominated his mind, being very distracting in conversation and during his waking hours. There were times when he closed his eyes and reverted to the comparative safety, as far as he was concerned, of blindness.

Why do I mention this? Because it seems to me that Mike May and his perseverance at integrating new experiences, at finding ways of coping with them and even using them to his advantage, provide us with a sensitive analogy. We might usefully bear him in mind when we are considering the selection of persons to be trained to become counsellors and psychotherapists in primary care. This is someone of courage, of boldness, someone who does not regress always into the old ways but recalls what he knows and is prepared to integrate his knowledge and skill into a new world. I grant you that the integration and coordination of knowledge, skills and ability is not all that unusual. What I want to emphasise is the addition of a new dimension that both excites and frustrates, and from which the primary care counsellor does not run away; instead, like the Captain of the Starship *Enterprise*, he or she 'boldly goes' into this new world. The new world is *The New NHS – Modern, Dependable* (Department of Health, 1997).

Desirable Characteristics of Trainees to Become Primary Care Counsellors

How do we select trainees for such a venture? How do we select counsellors to work in this domain? What are the characteristics that we need to look out for? I suggest to you that trainers need to be on the lookout for the following sort of people, some of whose characteristics I have already mentioned in my analogies:

- People with the desire to integrate theory, practice and experience.
- People with a lack of 'preciousness' and a curiosity about the way that others work.
- People with a collaborative spirit, who enjoy working along-

side others who have different approaches, and enjoy communicating with others at all levels.

- People who are keen to apply new learning and to evaluate and log their effectiveness; that is, those who take seriously continuous professional development as a professional and ethical obligation. Note that this is also a requirement of clinical governance.
- People who are tolerant of others, not only in their client work but also within their world of work, and who can cope with tensions and the demands of constant change.
- People who are robust in the face of adversity and able to be champions for their profession within their workplace.
- Last but not least, we need candidates who have had good training that has been rigorous, are grounded in the art and craft of counselling and are mature in their outlook; who have good rounded personalities with a sense of humour, a characteristic they will certainly need in this milieu. In other words, human beings who have had the best training available from a reputable course.

Selection Criteria and Process

If you haven't already realised, the sort of person of whom I am speaking is already a graduate to diploma level on a British Association for Counselling and Psychotherapy/United Kingdom Counsel for Psychotherapy (BACP/UKCP) approved course or the equivalent. It may well be that someone on a diploma course has already had a placement in primary care and there are guidelines issued by Faculty for Healthcare Counsellors and Psychotherapists (FHCP) on such matters (Seber and Sharman, 2004), and so the transition to primary care counselling trainee may proceed smoothly. However, the ideal type of person that I am thinking of is entering into work as a primary care counsellor having already achieved the current basic qualification as a counsellor.

I did use the word 'ideal'. Where are we going to get such an ideal candidate? Of course, despite every advance in psychometric testing, and every development in interviewing techniques for trainers, I do not believe that there is any 'fail-safe' way of selecting the perfect candidate. Therefore, what do I suggest? Nothing startling, simply a probationary period where our new trainee primary care counsellor is observed during practice and additional postgraduate training. What may be startling in this world of 'widening participation' in educational institutions is that there may be occasions when both the employer and the institution and perhaps a counselling supervisor will offer feedback to the effect that someone is not suited to this work. These days this takes courage but if we are going to have a credible service of quality within the NHS and one that reflects the best of our profession, this nettle will have to be grasped. Regular reports, appraisal and feedback, along with opportunities for the development of a new counsellor coming to work in primary care, are necessities. I am thinking especially of those occasions when a certain blindness sets in and, as for Mike May, eyes become closed and regression to former ways becomes a habit.

Postgraduate Training for Counsellors in Primary Care

What I offer to you for your consideration is the candidate whom it is desirable to employ as a counsellor in primary care. It is also the sort of person who (besides having the perfection of the Archangel Gabriel) will desire to have that additional training that is so necessary for anyone seriously expecting a career in counselling in the NHS, let alone primary care. A trainer will also be looking for all of the characteristics that I have mentioned previously in applicants for postgraduate courses for counsellors working in the NHS or primary care.

What might be the content of a postgraduate course for counsellors working in the NHS? In recent years, a great deal has been written concerning the subjects that need to be covered by those whose career path takes them into the NHS, and especially primary care, where the majority of mental health distress is contained and, it is hoped, alleviated. The pioneering work of Penny Henderson and the Counselling in Primary Care Trust (Henderson, 1995) and the work of the Counselling in Medical Settings (now the FHCP) Division of the then BAC (British Association for Counselling), now BACP, has to be acknowledged in this regard. The work has been refined over the years but remains substantially the same. In 2002 the Counselling and Psychotherapy Forum for Primary Care published them on its website.

Course Content for a Postgraduate Counselling in Primary Care Course

For those of you who are not familiar with the recommendations that the Counselling in Primary Care Forum agreed and published on its website, I offer you some extracts from the Forum document. First, the basic training that I have already mentioned is laid out in general terms: 450 hours covering core theoretical model(s) and skills training. This level of training needs to be acceptable to the relevant professional bodies and will also lead to accreditation/registration with BACP/CPC/UKCP.

It is suggested that training courses, which prepare people for work in the NHS include:

- assessment (mental health risk);
- ethics;
- general legal issues;
- 40 hours minimum of personal development (this means individual personal therapy);
- 100 hours minimum of managed and supervised clinical placement.

There is nothing new here other than to note those three concerns that the Forum had about basic training courses, where there is a lack of discussion of and input on the assessment of clients in general terms and the recognition of *mental* illness. Note the term 'recognition', not 'diagnosis', of mental illness. Counsellors are not qualified to diagnose, but they need to be able to assess clients, assess risk and know when a client is suffering from a mental illness, and to be fully aware of the limits to their competency.

Similarly, there needs to be a capacity to work with ethical principles. It is expected that most counsellors will be aware of the BACP Ethical Framework. It is vital in our pluralistic society for a counsellor to be able to think ethically and to process issues as they arise. This is obviously important in the arena of primary care and needs to be integrated with NHS procedures and protocols. There is a BACP information sheet on *The Ethical Framework for Good Practice in Counselling and Psychotherapy within the NHS* by Peter Cardew (2005). Finally, there needs to be an appreciation of legal matters and how they affect a counsellor's work.

Recommendations concerning specialist postgraduate training for counsellors working in the NHS have been made by the Counselling and Psychotherapy Forum for Primary Care. These have been adopted by the Faculty for Healthcare Counsellors and Psychotherapists and the Association for Counsellors and Psychotherapists in Primary Care.

Specialist Training

In addition to generic training, those desirous of working in the NHS need to add the following items:

- NHS structure and policy;
- clinical governance;
- NHS multidisciplinary working;

- knowledge of mental health referral pathways and procedures;
- medication;
- focused, evidence-based practice;
- audit, evaluation and research.

This additional training may be acquired through taught models and/or clinical experience.

The Counselling in Primary Care Forum considered all the above additional training components as vital for any counsellors working in the NHS. It really is necessary for counsellors working in primary care to immerse themselves into the NHS and to attempt to understand the machinations and working of this immense health machine. This is more than understanding the dynamics of a large group; it is, in effect, a whole new culture and a culture that is constantly undergoing change and development at a considerable rate of knots. Many counsellors are all for a quiet life and if this is the case then the NHS is not the place to work. Ignorance of the workings of the NHS cannot be a defence for those working within it because the NHS is overflowing with freely available information, especially via its website (www.doh.gov.uk). Counsellors need to engage with the culture and the new thinking that is constantly emerging, not uncritically but with a certain acceptance that change will always be occurring.

It goes without saying that clinical governance is a necessary ingredient in any primary care counsellor's work and again it needs to be understood and appreciated as a regulator of quality in standards and performance.

The notion of independent working is not for the primary care or NHS counsellor. Collaboration is the name of the game, with all its joys and benefits as well as its unfulfilled expectations. This is not to say that professional autonomy is not to be sought – it is, but not at the expense of a lack of collaboration with colleagues in the NHS team. Credibility is to be sought not only with patients but also with our colleagues in other health professions.

Training will be further enhanced by an understanding of mental health referral pathways and procedures both within and outside the NHS. Knowing what others do and how they work is essential. The *Healthcare Counselling and Psychotherapy Journal*, is useful to NHS and primary care counsellors because one of its aims is to further that understanding between disciplines and know where we can, together, help others.

It is obvious to those working within primary care that not all patients referred for counselling have eschewed the use of medication to ease their emotional or physical distress. It is important that primary care counsellors know and understand the commonly prescribed medication and that if they are counselling someone with a physical complaint they can check out the potential effects of that medication on mood, presentation and capacity for engagement in therapy. Collaboration and communication with the client's GP or practice nurse is a necessity.

The last two items of essential specialist training are both focused on the integration of audit, evaluation and research and the application of all of this into good counselling practice. NHS guidelines and clinical governance demand that all NHS practitioners of all disciplines relate to an evidence base and incorporate that knowledge into practice wherever possible. Counselling still has a long way to go in demonstrating that it is a discipline with integrity that is backed up by credible research. It behoves all those who see counselling in the NHS as a career to contribute positively to this and to acquire, where possible, some basic skills. It is desirable that counsellors go beyond this by contributing to that necessary research. There is a longstanding debate about the difficulties and the difference in the philosophical basis of the more holistic approach of therapy compared with the medical model and the hierarchies of evidence used by the National Institute for Clinical Excellence (NICE). The need to be more acquainted with research and its application is essential.

Conclusion

All of the above comprises the specialist training that is essential for an NHS/primary care counsellor. It may be acquired through continuing professional development (CPD) and this is particularly relevant using the knowledge and skills framework established by Agenda for Change (Department of Health, 2004). It may be acquired through institutions of higher and further education or specialist agencies. Wherever it takes place, *the request is that it does take place* for the benefit of the counselling profession and above all for the benefit of NHS patients. These are the basics without which counsellors in primary care will not become the essential component that we believe counsellors are in the New NHS.

I have not mentioned training in counselling for particular conditions or circumstances: for example, depression, relationships, systems theory, miscarriage, bereavement. There is information and training aplenty on such things. I emphasise the need for specific training to work in primary care and the NHS. The need is for counsellors and their trainers who wish to work in the NHS to realise that there is a new dimension here that brings particular challenges. Counselling makes a distinctive contribution to the NHS (Eatock and Rusello, 2004). To return to my introduction, there is a need for us to live and work as counsellors in this other world for the benefit of our society and, when we know that we are skiing down the slope, not to close our eyes.

References

Cardew, P. (2005) BACP Information sheet DG10, *The Ethical Framework for Good Practice in Counselling and Psychotherapy within the NHS*. Rugby: British Association for Counselling and Psychotherapy.

Department of Health (1997) *The New NHS – Modern, Dependable*. London: The Stationery Office.

Department of Health (2004) *Agenda for Change*. London: The Stationery Office.

Eatock, J. and Rusello, A. (2004) The distinctive contribution of counselling/psychotherapy to health and healthcare in Britain. *Healthcare Counselling and Psychotherapy Journal*, 4(3).

Guardian (2003) Mike May's dairy. *Guardian*, 26 August, G2.

Henderson, P. (1995) *Counselling in Primary Care Trust*. Staines.

Seber, P. H. and Sharman, K. (2004) *Guidance for Best Practice: The Employment of Counsellors and Psychotherapists in the NHS*. Rugby: British Association for Counselling and Psychotherapy.

CHAPTER FIVE

What Is Appropriate Training?

An External Examiner's View of Training

Douglas Hooper

IN Chapter Six Penny Henderson outlines the way in which the first postgraduate training for would-be counsellors in primary care settings was developed. At an early stage I agreed that I would act as external examiner to the original seven courses and also undertake the task of assessing the progress of the courses on behalf of the Counselling in Primary Care Trust. Obviously the universities and colleges had to agree that I would occupy both roles – which seemed neatly complementary – and without exception they agreed to this arrangement. Later, when the first courses were under way, four more courses asked me to take on the role of external examiner alone, to which I agreed. These experiences, then, have extended from 1996 to 2004 and have encompassed monitoring the work of more than 300 post-graduate students in college settings varying from prestigious universities to colleges of higher education. Their location was also widespread, extending from Scotland to the south coast of England.

I had an unrivalled opportunity to monitor students, teachers and college organisations in a comparative way that was very uncommon in this kind of appraisal. But this encompassed by no means all of the centres teaching some aspect of counselling/ psychotherapy in primary health care. As a result of a survey conducted by Penny Henderson on behalf of the Forum (Henderson, 2000), 68 courses were identified within the milieu of the British Association for Counselling and Psychotherapy course directory, which offered teaching in the area. These were examined to see how closely they came to the Forum outline syllabus: the minimum training standards and person specification criteria (Counselling and Psychotherapy Forum for Primary Care, 2001a, b) that had been developed. The review revealed that only 25 of the 68 were broadly teaching to that standard. About those, of course, we know nothing in detail. Clearly a potential student may, or may not, know whether any given course meets the Forum criteria for course material, teaching, and course organisation.

The courses with which I was involved all conformed to the Forum proposals and especially the initial seven, because it was from their mutual experiences that the Forum syllabus was created. But these were designed in conjunction with a large conference in 1999 in which I laid out my view of what we should regard as quality and excellence in the teaching and practice of counselling in this particular field of work (Hooper, 1999).

In that paper I delineated the characteristics that, I believed, summarised the standards to which we should aspire. These encompassed a number of parameters of work that, taken together, would result in practice excellence. These were all based on a competent and effective theory and knowledge base in psychological therapies.

In detail they were:

- That practice must be focused on primary care context needs. These include responding to the referral within the primary care context with the knowledge that other health professionals will also be involved with the client. This is significantly different from both freelance private practice and secondary mental health care systems.

- That the practice used should be multi-modal and not rely on one theory and practice model. The emphasis of the therapy is on working with the patients' presenting problems and using whatever techniques are appropriate.
- Recognition by the counsellor/therapist that work in primary care with clients is episodic. The client/patient normally has a long-term relationship with the practice and often with a particular GP, and counselling will form part of an evolving treatment pattern.
- Discriminating as to who can and who cannot benefit from the therapy available and also the contextual frame for the counselling.
- To be alive to and abreast of both therapeutic service developments and general developments in the primary care resource.
- Developing a healthy self-reflexive mode in both evaluation and development, valuing the work of the therapeutic self as well as the contribution of the team members.

Given this initial set of principles, what kind of education and training would be appropriate for the production of a competent practitioner? We need to dwell here on the word 'appropriate': the *Oxford English Dictionary* defines 'appropriate' as follows: 'Inherent; characteristic; specially suitable for; *proper and fitting*' (my emphasis). Note also that the concept of education is here as well as that of 'training' – the title commonly used in preparing counsellors and therapists. This advanced practice (for that is what it is) needs to be bedded in both sound conceptual understanding and a clear appreciation and facility in the acquisition of appropriate skills. The counsellor/therapist working in the primary care setting will be expected to deal with a wide range of presenting problems, varying in both severity and context. The competent practitioner needs a good wide-ranging understanding of the problem areas but set into a conceptual framework that enables the therapist to place the problem and the corresponding work to be done.

The next question, then, is: what is a proper and fitting course that will result in the sound and confident practitioner outlined above? As a result of examining both the students and courses that have been developed and taught, certain areas of teaching stand out as being both proper and fitting and therefore appropriate to the task of preparing the practitioner.

1 The teaching should be at the postgraduate level. This was often difficult for the students I examined to achieve but I believe vital for the counsellor/therapist to develop the necessary personal competence to practise in the complex multidisciplinary primary care team. Not only does this level challenge the student, it also provides her with an appropriate status. I profoundly disagree with those who argue that this level of learning is not required by the journeywoman ordinary practitioner in primary care.
2 The framework for the teaching and learning must be that of general medical practice. An understanding of the generic issues in counselling and psychotherapy in broad health care is not enough. Health/illness is an enormous business operating on a variety of levels in multiple contexts. We now require a doctor to undertake three years of postgraduate training for primary care practice and the psychological practitioner needs similarly to be properly prepared for the context.
3 The practice teaching should be proper and fitting for the problems presented by patients who come to the primary care setting for help. This is often a dilemma for counsellors. The expectation of the referring doctor or other professional might be for a problem-solving approach to the presenting problems. Counsellors and therapists are trained in their core work to address the client and not necessarily the presenting

problem. Further, people frequently present their problems to a GP dressed up as a pattern of physical ill-health. Although the GP may recognise that the person's disarray in life is psychosocial rather than physical, it may be uncomfortable for the patient to accept this. So the would-be therapist in the primary care setting must learn to accept the problem initially as the person presents it and move towards a reframing of the problems. This is a sophisticated approach that may require the student to do some *unlearning* first of all.

4 Training and education must also be proper and fitting for the student. At present the vast majority of therapists wishing to work in primary care are mature women with significant generic experience. Over 90 per cent of the students whom I have examined fit this description – although this may now be changing. The students in the examined courses, however, brought both significant life experience and practice experience to the postgraduate setting. However, their earlier formal learning may have been undertaken some years ago. Where this is the case they will need teaching that recognises their current status as well as challenging their practice. These issues were recognised early on by the tutors organising the first wave of courses. Some institutions, indeed, abandoned a one-year programme after the first year for a two-year programme because the students needed the extra year to reposition themselves and their practice. For these students academic challenge is apposite, but not academic pedantry.

5 The training and education must be proper and fitting for the multidisciplinary context in which the therapy will take place. A counsellor/therapist may well be operating in a primary care context with up to ten other health practitioners, a number of whom may have some input into the care of the particular patient. This can easily be continuing while the psychological work is proceeding, particularly for people with chronic health problems, known colloquially as 'heart sink' patients. It is, of course, possible (and bad practice) for

the counsellor to appear in the practice, see the individual and then disappear again without initiating a wider reflexive practice. This may be the student's way to protect himself or herself against what he or she may judge as interference with his or her way of working. It is of course very important to sustain the confidentiality required in ethical practice. But the balance is difficult and students need much help to learn how to practise successfully in the multidisciplinary setting. Educationally this means introducing the work of other health professionals to counsellors in interactive seminar approaches – and vice versa.

6 The learning must be appropriate to the rigour of evaluation. In medical care generally, evidence-based practice is seen as most desirable. Led by the National Institute for Clinical Excellence (NICE), single therapies such as many drug regimes seem to lead themselves easily to this approach. This has included the support by NICE for the single approach of cognitive-behavioural therapy. Evaluation of other psychological approaches is difficult to fit to this model and there are some important modifications that should be made to any attempt to evaluate psychological therapies. Yet despite this caveat it is very appropriate to students that they should adopt a rigorous approach to case-oriented evaluation. Generally counsellors and psychotherapists are not comfortable with 'research'. However, the CORE system of counselling evaluation was actually developed in the practice of the first groups of students in the early primary care courses and has now been used widely. Thus the principles of sound evaluation are a proper and fitting study for people planning to work in the critical general practice environment.

7 Finally, it is appropriate that students working at a postgraduate level should expect to be both recognised as skilled practitioners and properly rewarded for their work. A number of people have lobbied vigorously for this level of recognition and in the Agenda for Change NHS managers have agreed to

recognise formally the practitioners involved who are not psychologists or child psychotherapists. These two groups already had formal recognition. Development of the position certainly depends in part on the standing of the course itself and can only be built over time – something that unfortunately has not always been the case. The graduating students I have examined certainly have a competent professional persona as a result of their work, especially where the course itself has become well regarded.

Issues Arising for Future Education and Training Programmes

Taken together, these characteristics of excellent practice and the concepts of appropriate training for this counselling role complement each other. Elsewhere in this book we discuss the detail of *what* should be in the curriculum for a course that is usually part-time and extending over two years. The examination of the students demonstrates that to enable the student to become an excellent practitioner in the primary care context does require a significant amount of new learning as well as a sharp reorientation from previous learning and practice.

With the expansion in numbers and expertise of the counsellors/psychotherapists, practitioners should become organisationally more secure, and other patterns of training will probably emerge. If the career path is seen by students as being more secure and predictable than it has been in the past, then there could be a demand for courses that prepare the student for professional working in the primary care setting right from the beginning. This could be done by a tailored course, or alternatively by introducing significant learning modules alongside more generic material. What is also clear from the early experiences is that working in this environment is most certainly not simply transposing existing levels of skill and experience to a new context – a practice that commonly occurred in the past and is probably still happening.

For the primary care service, the clients and the practice of counselling/psychotherapy, appropriate levels of competent practice are vital. It is far better to have fewer practitioners all of whom are efficient and effective than a greater number less well prepared, particularly as the outcome of these approaches will continue to be judged on both effectiveness and efficiency grounds by employers and colleagues alike. The proposals by Lord Layard (2004) are for dramatically increased numbers of practitioners specially trained in cognitive-behavioural therapy, but we should be cautious about the training programmes needed to bring this about. Such programmes need to be grounded firmly in the way we have already suggested, but, from an employment point of view in line with current Department of Health thinking, it is clearly important for student practitioners following the course outline we suggest also to be properly trained and informed about cognitive-behavioural therapy.

The issue of quality of practice relates directly, of course, to the quality of the preparatory teaching. The Forum has taken a significant initiative by publishing the minimum standards that it believes are required, but there is no way at present in which the course providers can be judged themselves. This is a wider problem. In recent years counselling and psychotherapy courses have proliferated, in many cases without any control over their quality and safety. The British Association for Counselling and Psychotherapy and the United Kingdom Council for Psychotherapy have set standards for those colleges etc. who wish to be accredited by them. This helps but it does little or nothing to prevent any teaching group from setting up and offering courses to students outside this remit.

This is not only the case for broad-based teaching. In addition, under the rubric of these organisations there is little or no appraisal of any specialist training of the kind with which we are concerned. The Faculty of Healthcare Counselling of the British Association does give guidance, but does not itself approve specialist courses in any area of health care. In the experimental days of the Primary Care Trust sponsored courses, there was some internal control through the consortium of tutors meeting with people appointed by the Trust, such as myself, Penny Henderson and Graham Curtis-Jenkins, but this is no longer in place. So there is a hiatus between the education and training programmes and the employers of people prepared by these programmes.

This can be met by the service providers in the NHS being aware of the Forum minimum standards document either directly or by taking advice from informed people or organisations (such as the Network of Service Providers – see Chapter Fourteen by Jane Rosoman) about course provision. Perhaps in the long run, the service providers will provide would-be counsellors in primary health care with a list of training organisations that they approve. Alternatively, the Health Professions Council could or should take on this role in order to approve practitioners for listing by the Council.

The experience gained from the examination of the students from the first tranche of courses showed that there are significant issues for students and teachers alike in delivering good quality training and education in this area of work. The need for students was to graduate at an advanced level so that they had professional standing that would be respected by other health professionals. The respect came from a wide grasp of the therapeutic issues involved in primary care work, which the students had integrated into their previous learning. The burden of this chapter – and of this book – is that the groundwork is now done. The important findings from that work must be carried through into the programmes that will emerge in order to continue to meet the needs of primary care in the coming years.

References

Counselling and Psychotherapy Forum for Primary Care (2001a) *Minimum Training Standards for Primary Care Counselling*. Brighton: Counselling and Psychotherapy Forum for Primary Care.

Counselling and Psychotherapy Forum for Primary Care (2001b) *Person Specification Criteria*. Brighton: Counselling and Psychotherapy Forum for Primary Care.

Henderson, P. (2000) A study of training provision in primary healthcare counselling in the UK. Brighton: Counselling and Psychotherapy Forum for Primary Care.

Hooper, D. (1999) The pursuit of excellence. In *Quality, Standards and Excellence. Setting Standards for Education, Training and Professional Development of Counsellors and Psychotherapists in Primary Care, Conference Proceedings*. Brighton: Counselling and Psychotherapy Forum for Primary Care.

Layard, Lord R. (2004) *Mental Health: Britain's Biggest Social Problem?* (available from www.strategy.gov.uk/downloads/files/mh_layard. pdf).

CHAPTER SIX

Training Counsellors to Work in Primary Care

Penny Henderson

I HAVE been thinking about training counsellors to work in primary care for the past ten years, and have created, and been a party to developing, ideas about what is required and how such requirements might be delivered. This chapter details three different course designs, a 1995 curriculum, the recommendations of the Counselling and Psychotherapy Forum for Primary Care (referred to as 'the Forum') and a low-key alternative for initially qualified counsellors that emphasises robust arrangements for continuous professional development through peer and supervisory review and a portfolio. There is little essential disagreement between the first two designs, except for the elements that mark the great developments there have been in counselling in primary care between the 1995 curriculum and the 2001 Forum recommendations.

This reflection about training covers a period that has seen major changes in the delivery of counselling services in primary care. In 1995 the training challenges entailed the development of skills and understanding about working short term, or to given time limits, a concept largely new to a majority of counsellors in all contexts, understanding how to work with the diverse range of patients who are referred and the thorny issues that were then countercultural to counselling norms: working as part of a team and sustaining appropriate levels of confidentiality within such work.

Today's challenges relate to evidence-based medicine and its consequences: using more assessment and audit tools (such as CORE;[1] more about this further on in this chapter), developing a range of skills including some familiarity with cognitive-behavioural therapy (CBT) approaches and more collaborative work that invites counsellors to see themselves as part of a team of mental health workers in primary care. Current developments regarding mental health in primary care focus on issues of social inclusion for all patients and the integration of care pathways, which include counselling as one of a series of possible options for patients who may also be offered self-help packages, guided reading and access to other psychological services. Understanding partnership, then, is a key for qualified counsellors.

Any curriculum must cover more than a list of knowledge, or skill development. Personal and professional development, progress in ethical thinking and self-awareness gained through personal development groups or therapy is essential in initial training courses. Continuing professional development (CPD) is an essential part of post-qualifying practice. Even in managed services, the need is great for individuals to be confident that they can review their own efficacy through the habits of reflective practice.

Despite the unique demands on counsellors of working in this context, which would imply that further post-qualifying training is essential, current employment patterns disincline the majority of counsellors from pursuing substantive courses; hence the design 3 option described below.

Design 1: The 1995 Curriculum – MA Developed by the Counselling in Primary Care Trust

Background

In the mid-1990s, it was estimated that 25 per cent of GP practices employed counsellors (Addington Hall et al., 1993). The Counselling in Primary Care Trust (CPCT) was highly significant in influencing and supporting the extension of counselling in this setting through research, networking and financial support for developments in training and research. In this period, counsellors from an extremely wide range of backgrounds and training were individually negotiating their place in primary care teams, and they developed a range of services and interventions. Some were barely qualified and even unsupervised. Others moved across from nursing, occupational therapy, other health related professions, Relate or social work. Many traditions of teamwork, in particular, influenced the structure and practice at the time.

Because there was no national statutory or regulatory certifying body, doctors found it difficult to recruit counsellors whom they could be confident were appropriately trained to work in a primary care setting. Some publications attempted to remedy this (Counselling in Medical Settings Division, 1993; CPCT, 1994) and to identify the training needs of counsellors to work in this setting (Curtis Jenkins et al., 1992). The survey by Curtis Jenkins et al. discovered that no counsellor-training organisation in the UK in 1991 was offering any training on an initial course specifically for counsellors who wished to work in primary care. Some basic training courses did have trainee placements in these settings, but frequently without recruiting supervisors who had direct knowledge of the demands of work in this context, or experience of supervising brief counselling.

A further study into the training needs of counsellors was completed (Curtis Jenkins et al., 1995). The in-depth semi-structured survey questionnaire completed by counsellors working in primary care revealed that respondents, many with years of experience and extra training, considered they had considerable gaps in their knowledge and skills that hindered the development of the services they sought to provide. The information the survey questionnaire produced was used to develop the course described below.

One Solution: The Core with Options Model 1995

The aim was to design a diploma for qualified and experienced counsellors who might already be working in a primary health care setting. It was essential to do three things:

1. To structure the course around a core of common gaps identified through research.
2. To recognise the knowledge and experience students already had and capitalise on that by using peer consultation, feedback and assessment methods.
3. To allow them to choose some options to address individual gaps in their initial training and experience and extend their knowledge and skill.

The course design therefore emphasised students' contribution to their own practice development, and allowed one-third of the time for optional modules and assessment, and two-thirds for a core syllabus. It is important to say immediately that this design was never implemented like this, as training institutions could not reasonably organise their teaching this way. However, the ideas were influential in encouraging the trainers to cover what they could in the time they had.

Developing the Core Syllabus

The CPCT research (Curtis Jenkins et al., 1995) identified topics and skills that counsellors then working in GP practices considered either an essential or a desirable basis for counselling in primary care. Each respondent noted how far his or her own initial counselling training covered these matters. This research identified 11 key elements that, at that time, had often been missing in initial counsellor training:

1. Training in the medical model(s).
2. Medication and its effects.
3. The structure of the National Health Service.
4. Preparation for the range of patient problems brought to counselling.
5. Training in brief therapy models.
6. Team collaboration.
7. Managing the waiting list.
8. How to set up a counselling practice in a primary care setting.
9. Training in specific disorders (e.g. eating disorders, sexual abuse).
10. Guidance on appropriate and inappropriate referrals for counselling in primary care, and on creating a referral network to secondary care.
11. Help to cope with the isolation the counsellors were feeling in this setting.

This list was focused on three major gaps that a post-qualifying diploma course should address:

- working in multidisciplinary teams in a primary health care setting, with a developed understanding of the constantly changing NHS context;
- developing models of health and illness that clarified the potential counselling roles in primary health care;
- developing an understanding of models of time-effective therapy, and skills to work with clients in short time frames but on a continuing basis (paralleling the role of the GP).

For each of these broad areas, a syllabus was developed that reflected the knowledge, skill and personal development required to reach a level of competency considered appropriate to work effectively in this setting.

Students were encouraged to negotiate appropriate agreements with their GP employers about the target group to whom counselling would preferentially be offered (e.g. patients over the age of 16 with depression, anxiety or relationship difficulties, employment-related stresses or self-esteem issues, or who are having difficulties coming to terms with a medical diagnosis or condition). It was considered important for counsellors in primary care to be skilled in a range of ways to work because counselling may be offered to individuals, couples, families or groups. If group work to address issues of anxiety, stress management, bereavement, or relationship difficulties, or health education and life change issues, was to be offered, courses were encouraged to include training for it during their course.

The syllabus of this course is outlined in Appendix 5.

The Assumptions Underlying Course Design

The assumptions about what makes for effective learning at this level of counselling training were that:

1 Students learn best when they are active learners; and they will become more rigorously reflective practitioners as they develop their capacity for self-monitoring.

2 Awareness of self is a key prerequisite for becoming an effective and reflective practitioner. The students' most important resources are personality, self-awareness and capacity to reflect and to apply theory effectively. This meant that the course design had to be sufficiently integrative of theory, skill and personal development that this awareness was extended to:
   - motivation to work in a primary care setting;
   - how students use their professional support system;

- whether students' own intimacy needs are adequately met outside of the counselling relationships;
- attitudes to authority, power and the allocation of scarce resources;
- capacity to monitor and manage their own energy levels and habits of somatisation;
- capacity to use focus and boundaries appropriately with clients;
- interest in theory and the capacity to apply it;
- awareness of team, group and/or organisational dynamics.

3 Students must be robust enough to engage in a challenging combination of theoretical learning, skill development and personal development.

4 The development of skill in practice is essential to increased competence, and reflection on practice, which requires a sensitive combination of support and challenge from supervisor, mentor, tutors and peers, is essential to professional and skill development.

Optional Modules

In addition, a series of 12-hour optional training modules would be offered, from which each student must choose two. The working assumption was that all counsellors should be competent in all the following areas, but most counsellors will already be competent in some:

- working with systems (family and other);
- working with post-traumatic stress;
- group work in primary care (running time-limited groups and being a contact point for self-help groups);
- loss, bereavement and complicated grief;
- sexuality;
- working with couples.

In practice, although the idea was good, the exigencies of course organisation meant that this element was adapted in different ways by each course provider.

Course Outcomes

The courses were developed within a number of university and private institutions. A facilitated consortium of tutors met twice yearly over several years. This provided an innovative supportive and monitoring structure, which encouraged tutors to share their own developments and discuss difficulties with an exciting and unusual degree of openness. Douglas Hooper was external assessor for all the courses. However, once the funding support of CPCT had finished, many of the courses did not recruit, and were either subsumed within other masters courses or disappeared. The same recruitment difficulty has dogged many subsequent courses. Many more have been developed and offered than have run.

Design 2: The Forum Proposal – Minimum Training Standards[2]

The Counselling and Psychotherapy Forum for Primary Care was convened as described elsewhere in this book, and organised consultation days with training providers to identify good practice guidelines for training to work in this setting. The Forum commissioned more questionnaire-based research into diploma-level and post-qualifying training in 2000, to see whether it more fully met the needs of their graduates who might want to work in primary care (Henderson, 2000).

Five existing specialist training courses returned pilot questionnaires and all of these covered the identified curriculum, which had been derived, once more, from the research already quoted, and further studies by Burton et al. (2001) and Scott (2000, 2001). All the specialist courses expected students to be working or have a placement in primary care, and in one case the supervisors were required to have experience of primary care. Then 68 BACP-accredited diploma courses were sent a modified questionnaire, and 25 responded (37 per cent, a low response). A major surprise was the huge variation among BACP-accredited courses, which indicated that it could not be taken for granted that these courses equip graduates for future work in primary care, through either their curriculum or their placement experiences. Interestingly, there was no agreement on curriculum priorities even between courses with the same theoretical orientation. Yet a number of professional bodies accept an initial diploma as an adequate preparation, according to Burton et al. (2001). These diploma courses generally now do teach about mental illness, legal issues and sexual issues, which was less common in 1995, but still insufficiently cover assessment for brief therapy, audit or outcome assessment and knowledge of the current NHS structure, psychosomatic conditions, mental health referral pathways and psychotropic medication.

In 2001 the Forum published recommendations for training for counsellors in primary care. This was the product of much thought and negotiation benefiting from input from people representing the counselling and psychotherapy organisations, training institutions and other interested parties. Members shared an expectation that statutory regulation would soon make appropriate levels of training mandatory, and wished to be in a position to make sound recommendations. Despite differing theoretical orientations, agreement was finally reached on this outline.

Key Recommendations about Training that Is Necessary Prior to Work in Primary Care

A primary care counsellor should have had an *initial* generic counselling training for 450 hours to match accreditation norms in BACP and CPC. This training should have had some emphasis on core theoretical model(s) and some skills training. To be suitable preparation for working in the NHS this training should include:

- assessment (including mental health and risk management);
- ethical frameworks for professional practice;
- general legal issues;
- working with diversity.

In addition, 40 hours minimum of personal therapy and 100 hours of managed and supervised clinical placement were named a necessary prerequisite part of initial training.

This shift of emphasis from the 1995 curriculum described above demonstrates the big changes that had taken place in many initial counsellor training course in the eight years since the original curriculum: working with diversity and having a good grasp of assessment and legal issues had been very variably included in initial training in the former, and were considered essential seven years later.

Specialist Counselling Training

The protocol continued: 'In addition to the above, those seeking employment within the NHS need to include in their continuing professional development (CPD):

- NHS structure and policy;
- clinical governance;
- NHS multidisciplinary working;
- knowledge of mental health referral pathways and procedures;
- psychotropic medication;
- focused, evidence-based practice;
- time-limited therapy;
- audit, evaluation and research;
- notes/confidentiality and the law.'

This list highlights the growing impact of clinical governance, evidence-based practice and audit, evaluation and research in this context. The increasing integration of counselling into the work of the surgery and the community mental health team has led to more emphasis on understanding legal issues, especially around child protection. More counsellors now write reports for legal teams or contribute to doctors' reports for housing applications, refugee status or access to other services. Concepts of appropriate confidentiality when working in primary care have shifted radically in this period, and each counsellor has to work out how to collaborate appropriately with colleagues while retaining an explicit level of client confidentiality as appropriate to each patient and surgery.

The Forum debates about how counsellors should access and develop this knowledge, skill and understanding veered between recommending post-qualifying courses and accepting that courses that had been offered had not run for lack of applicants. Creative realistic proposals were necessary. Thus the Forum recommended that 'this [the list above] may be acquired through taught CPD modules and/or clinical experience validated by critical reflection and personal portfolio developments'.

At least one of the organisational members of the Forum, CPC, has offered individual training days in many of these topics for its members. Other providers, such as the Tavistock Clinic, offered a year-long course in 2005 for continuous professional development focusing on primary care issues for primary care counsellors. Many locally managed services provide in-service courses, and more may do so once resources have been allocated in the light of the Agenda for Change.

Agenda for Change has agreed job profiles and pay scales for NHS counsellors on a national basis that will encourage better integration and recognition of counselling. For more details of this see Chapter One in this volume.

Design 3: The Option of Supervised Practice Associated with Monitoring

Until all primary care counsellors are part of an integrated and managed service with coherently planned and implemented CPD for each counsellor, it may be that peer group learning or group supervision could be the location for more carefully documented and self-monitored reflection. Using a portfolio to identify learning needs and gaps, practitioners could record their learning about counselling in this context, and this could give some more direction and focus to their CPD. Identification of learning needs is now done with a supervisor or mentor during the BACP re-accreditation procedures, and this model could be used for all to monitor progress and to form the basis of an ongoing record for each individual counsellor. Reporting back to a supervisor or peer at defined intervals would encourage counsellors to review their plans, learning and achievements more rigorously.

As the first generation of primary care counsellors begin to retire, move into supervision or management of a service or move on, the second and third generations of counsellors in primary care face new challenges, including the changing structures of employment and support, the requirements of evidence-based practice and the pressure of waiting lists lengthened by GPs' increasing recognition of the value of counselling. It is important that all primary care counsellors work collaboratively with existing colleagues, GPs, CPNs, health visitors, midwives and new colleagues, like the psychology graduate mental health workers who are paid to provide access to useful books or protocols for self-assessment or for work with less complex cases. Sometimes psychology departments provide primary care psychology services within the surgery. Agreements need to be developed about which patients are to be referred to whom, and how training can be provided to encourage collaborative working rather than competition.

It is very important that counsellors in primary care have a good grasp of which clients they are competent to see within the time constraints of the service, and those whom they need to refer into the mental health system or out to voluntary bodies. This implies that they have some experience of serious and enduring mental illness. This option could be greatly strengthened if *every* newly appointed counsellor in primary care has – or has had – a supported placement on an admission ward in secondary mental health care for a significant period, ideally for a day a week over a period of months. This would inform the counsellor of colleagues and systems in the mental health referral pathways, and also clarify which patients may be unsuitable for brief therapy in primary care. This could be a *major* contributor to good risk assessment by primary care counsellors.

Similarly, some contact individually or in a group with mental health service users to discuss what users see as their needs and the limits of the services in meeting them would help the counsellors to see where they sit within the overall pattern of provision, and give them a more developed understanding of the stigmas and complexities of mental health diagnoses.

Increasingly, supervisors of counsellors in primary care are now people who were among the early generations of counsellors in this context, and they do have a good understanding of it, and of the pressures of working in time effective ways. This is also a change from 1998, when Burton et al. found in a survey of counsellors in primary care that 37 per cent of their supervisors were counsellors, and the rest were psychotherapists, counselling or clinical psychologists, social workers or psychiatrists. Only 25 per cent of these supervisors worked in primary care, and 75 per cent knew no doctor in the counsellor's practice. Many had no training in brief therapy. It is still rare, and may not necessarily be appropriate, for supervisors to know the surgery team, but where it happens, the opportunity arises for the supervisory relationship to support the counsellor to work in ways that also support colleagues and the team, and understand the priorities of the surgery or PCT.

In a small and unpublished survey of 20 counsellors in primary care in Cambridgeshire in 2001 (Henderson, 2001) respondents were asked how they had learned about topics commonly met in primary care: 'from their initial training, from experience, from CPD or from supervision'. Some ticked all the options for some topics, but replies suggest that supervision was a major source of learning.

Fewer than 20 per cent of respondents felt their initial training had prepared them for mental health assessment or risk assessment, termination of pregnancy and fertility issues, phobias, physical problems and addictions. Nine respondents noted they had learned about risk assessment and mental health assessment through supervision, CPD or professional experience. Most respondents (13 or 14 out of 20) felt they had learned from all the above sources about trauma and abuse, bereavement and loss, self-esteem, relationships, depression and anxiety. The latter are the most common foci of counselling in primary care.

In this group, 63 per cent said their supervisors had direct experience of primary care – a big shift in six years from the data of Burton et al. (1998). Such experienced supervisors are well placed to offer guidance on the practice of delivering the service in the changing NHS context.

In some areas psychology departments are helpful in providing training for primary care counsellors in CBT assessment and methodology, and even some ongoing supervision if counsellors wish to provide CBT counselling to patients within their surgeries. This can have the effect of informing both groups involved of the skills of the others.

NHS Developments

The National Institute for Clinical Excellence (NICE) publishes national guidelines for treatment within the NHS. Counsellors are now recognised as providers of appropriate care, but they are also expected to follow the guidelines, and to be able to give an account of the rationale for their 'treatment choices'. Such language is antithetical to some counselling trainings. Computer-literate counsellors can access the NICE guidelines – currently about depression and anxiety or self-harm, for example, at www.nice.org.uk. Increasingly they are expected to do so and to practise within the preferred interventions noted in the guidelines. Training implications therefore include both some computer literacy and confidence, and some willingness to review their practice in the light of the NICE guidelines and expectations of clinical governance. Clinical governance spells out that all services are to be delivered within standards set by professional self-regulation. Counsellors will also be expected to audit their work using one of the accepted methods such as CORE, developed by Mellor-Clark et al. at Leeds University, which includes brief forms completed by client and counsellor addressing the client's sense of well-being, problems, functioning and risk; or the Leeds MIND questionnaire, designed to elicit clients' feedback about their counselling.

Problems

One continuing area of difficulty is about practice placements in primary care for students on initial diploma courses. The Forum members were agreed that it is generally inadvisable for students to have placements in primary care at this stage unless there is another counsellor to act as mentor in the practice.

Fitzgerald and Murphy (1997) described the Derbyshire experiment to train counsellors for primary care *after* initial diploma training, and emphasised the value of another counsellor acting as a mentor in the practice in addition to a clinical supervisor. Often the mentor, or failing that role, the supervisor, acts as a linguistic interpreter between counselling language and the NHS mental health constructs. When counsellors are on placement in primary care, it is very important that the lines of accountability for their work are explicitly understood by all, and that they learn how to collaborate with colleagues trained in the different traditions of medicine, psychology and mental illness. (See Chapter Ten in this volume for a fuller discussion.)

At present the social class, ethnic and gender base of counsellors practising in primary care is too heavily weighted to those who can afford to earn low wages, to have insecure, frequently annual, contracts and to pay the substantial costs of counsellor training. Counsellors need to match the populations they serve and thus come from a wider ethnic and class range and include more men. It will not serve the counsellors or the service if the men who do enter counselling in primary care seem always to get the senior jobs. Greater diversity among counsellors will not appear until better systems of payment for training exist. Unlike colleagues in the team, psychologists, CPNs, doctors and nurses, the student counsellor's basic training as well as post-qualifying professional development are still commonly wholly self-funded. Too many primary care trusts and individual surgeries still have counsellors working in a voluntary unpaid, or poorly paid, capacity.

Until terms and conditions of employment are more secure, few counsellors will invest much in substantial post-qualifying training. Until there is some career path, it will continue to be a part of a patchwork of activities they engage in. Although this may keep them fresher than full-time work in primary care, it militates against them identifying themselves as a full part of the team in the surgery or as specialists within this context.

Concluding Comments

There is wide consensus on what counsellors in primary care need to know about and be able and resilient enough to do. There is broadly shared agreement about the value of ensuring that such counsellors have good assessment and referral skills and knowledge, and good skills in multidisciplinary working and brief therapy. It is almost unheard of now for any counsellor in primary care not to have supervision because of the requirements for membership of professional bodies.

Yet at present the jury is out among those who apply for these jobs, many of which are still for fewer than six hours a week at a rate of pay that no other psychological professional would consider, about how to provide access to training for them that fits in with their other commitments. They sustain their supervision, and are hungry for CPD and keen to attend training events with counselling colleagues or within the health service when and if they can be paid to attend. The next ten years may see a resolution through managed services so that they can work safely and so that patients are protected from practitioners working beyond their competence, or poorly integrated into a complex service. In general GPs are keen to hold on to their counsellors despite political and financial pressures not to. GPs may need to become advocates for them within the changing primary care trust system.

Notes

1 Clinical Outcomes for Routine Evaluation.

2 Please see Appendices 2 and 3 for the full Minimum Training Standards for Primary Care Counselling and Person Specification Criteria protocols.

References

Addington Hall, J., Brenneman, D., Freeling, P. and Sibbald, B. (1993) Counsellors in England and Welsh primary care: their nature and distribution. *British Medical Journal*, 29–33.

Burton, M., Curtis Jenkins, G. and Henderson, P. (1998) Primary care counsellors' experiences of supervision. *Counselling: The Journal of the British Association for Counselling*, 9(2), 122–33.

Burton, M., Mellor-Clark, J. and Simms-Ellis, R. (2001) *National Survey of Counsellors Working in Primary Care: Evidence for Growing Professionalism?* Occasional Paper 79. London: Royal College of General Practitioners.

Corney, R. and Jenkins, R. (1993) *Counselling in Primary Care*. London: Routledge.

Counselling in Medical Settings Division (1993) *Guidelines for the Employment of Counsellors Working in Primary Care*. Rugby: British Association for Counselling.

Counselling in Primary Care Trust (1994) *Information Booklet*. London: Counselling in Primary Care Trust.

Counselling and Psychotherapy Forum for Primary Care (2003a) *Minimum Training Standards for Primary Care Counselling*. Brighton: Counselling and Psychotherapy Forum for Primary Care.

Counselling and Psychotherapy Forum for Primary Care (2003b) *Person Specification Criteria*. Brighton: Counselling and Psychotherapy Forum for Primary Care.

Curtis Jenkins, G., Einzig, H. and Basharan, H. (1992) Training needs of counsellors working in primary medical care. The role of the training organisations. *CMS: News Journal of the British Association for Counselling*, 22, 9–13.

Curtis Jenkins, G., Einzig, H. and Basharan, H. (1995). The training needs of counsellors working in primary medical care. A survey questionnaire of counsellors working in primary care. *Journal of Mental Health*, 4, 205–9.

Daines, B., Gask, L. and Usherwood, T. (1997) *Medical and Psychiatric Issues for Counsellors*. London: Sage.

Fitzgerald, P. and Murphy, A. (1997) Counsellor training placements. *Medical Monitor*, May, 55–6.

Henderson, P. (2000) *A Study of Training Provision in Primary Healthcare Counselling in the UK*. Brighton: Counselling and Psychotherapy Forum in Primary Care.

Henderson, P. (2001) Unpublished research for Cambridgeshire Primary Care Trust.

Lemma, A. (1996) *Introduction to Psychopathology*. London: Sage.

MacLachlan, M. (1997) *Culture and Health*. Chichester: Wiley.

Rollnick, S., Mason, P. and Butler, C. (1999) *Health Behaviour Change*. London: Churchill Livingstone.

Scott, S. (2000) Vocational training of counsellors in primary care: what do GPs think? *Counselling in Practice*, 4(1).

Scott, S. (2001) Vocational training for counsellors, part 2. *Counselling in Practice*, 7(1).

CHAPTER SEVEN

Training for Competency

Finding the Right Course for Working in Primary Care

Michael Jacobs

THE rapid growth of counselling and of counselling courses from 1980 onwards has resulted in a bewildering choice, at least in some areas of the country, as to which course to attend. While it appears that there are many opportunities for employment as a counsellor, with the apparent expansion of counselling in the workplace and in primary care, to take just two examples, there are in fact many more counsellors in training than there are posts for them to fill. This makes it imperative that training is of the highest standard, one that will test the prospective counsellor, and assess him or her, as to whether or not he or she is likely to reach that point where competing for jobs has at least the possibility of some success. It may therefore be better in the long term to apply for a course that sets high standards of selection than to enrol for a locally advertised course, which takes anyone as a student, and which provides no real clue as to whether or not the student is likely to become a competent counsellor. This chapter suggests what the prospective student might look for in choosing whether or not to apply to a particular course.

Counselling is now available in over 80 per cent of general practices; it is frequently of a time-limited nature, and the work involves seeing a wide variety of ages and of presenting issues. A key feature of the work is the ability to assess which patients can best use the counselling contracts on offer, and sometimes how long the contract itself should be. It means working in a multidisciplinary setting, which means the ability to work cooperatively with other health care professionals, some of whom may be familiar with what counselling can offer and achieve, others of whom may be sceptical or even hostile to counselling. Thus, while a generic service is offered to patients, very specific skills are required, and particular knowledge of the setting is necessary. The question arises whether the courses that might offer training in generic counselling can also offer specific knowledge of the work of the primary care counsellor.

We have to recognise, of course, that in some areas of the country choice is more limited, with a local course that offers specific modules and training in primary care counselling being perhaps non-existent. In that situation questions of time and expense in travel arise, since a potential student should be asking: 'Has my local course a good reputation, and will it provide what I need to work in primary care? Or is it better to travel further afield in order to find one that will provide me with a better training, and enhanced opportunity for work after I graduate?' On the other hand, where there are a number of courses to choose from, the matter is complicated because it is likely that they will offer different syllabuses and espouse various counselling models (the difference between them perhaps at this stage meaning little or nothing to the interested applicant); and they may be accredited by different organisations, some of which are national bodies, others of which appear to suggest solid credentials for accrediting courses, but are not in fact specialist bodies or even national bodies.

Let us not mince words: there is some rivalry between courses, particularly where they are adjacent to each other; there is some rivalry between accrediting organisations; there is some rivalry between core models of counselling. The prospective student is therefore likely to be told by most courses that they are the best to attend, that their model is the most effective one and that their affiliations are the soundest. Let me warn you: your present author is tempted to do the same, promoting the accreditation of courses by BACP above all other bodies, preferring courses run in universities where there are further checks of quality and standards of teaching and assessment, and recommending courses where the model is in major part a psychodynamic one. Tempted, but not tempted enough, because such recommendations would be simplistic. I can think of courses that are not accredited by BACP, indeed may not be accredited by any body, that are worth applying for; I can think of university courses that may in some respects meet the requirements of the academic body in which they are situated, but fail to provide sufficient experience and training, however strong they are on academic education. I know that courses that have a person-centred core model can be just as comprehensive in their approach as psychodynamic courses, and that, despite my preference for psychodynamic theory as the core model, there are psychodynamic courses that are too narrow (in my opinion) to prepare students to work in the public arena. The prospective student needs to note paragraph 3.3 of the Minimum Training Standards document in Appendix 2, that theoretical models should fit patients, not the other way round. Beware of courses where only the core model is sufficient.

Some of these complexities need further explanation, related to the setting with which this book is concerned, primary care. If that is the setting in which the prospective student wishes eventually to work, as already indicated above, the chosen course must provide training and knowledge that will be necessary for that setting. I will spell that out in more detail. For example, much of the work in primary care counselling is what is called brief counselling or therapy, which in this context usually means a limit of between six and 12 'hour'-long sessions (the therapeutic hour often being 50 minutes). It is essential that this is a significant part of the course programme, not simply an add-on. Experience of brief work, and of assessment for brief work, is essential. Next, clients in primary care are of all ages from mid-adolescence onwards, and they will present issues that range from relationship problems to recognisable mental illness – so the course must not be limited to one age group, or cover only those issues with which generic counsellors are most at home. Referrals in primary care will vary, from doctors who understand what counsellors best work with, to 'dumping' heart-sink patients where there is little chance that brief counselling will be of any real help. Therefore courses must cover assessment, so that the primary care counsellor can distinguish how best to help and where referral may be necessary; and cover risk assessment, because there may be some referrals where it is unwise to work using particular methods. The starting point of any student therefore needs to be 'What do I need to learn?' as much as 'How good is this course?'

Documents produced by the Counselling and Psychotherapy Forum for Primary Care, which can be found in the appendices to this book, set out both the minimum training standards and the personal specification protocol for a primary care counsellor. Put together these recommendations suggest a number of key dimensions to a syllabus that are relevant to seeking placements and in due course employment in primary care. Does the course teach the skills not just of counselling, but also of brief counselling? Does it devote space to assessment of potential clients, to the limitations and possibilities for counselling in general and for brief counselling in particular? Does it cover risk assessment, for the welfare of both the client and the counsellor? Does it teach models of mental health and illness, together with possible explanations for issues that clients present (often known as psychopathology)? Does the course have at its heart recognition of issues of diversity: racial and cultural differences, gender and sexuality issues? Does the course engage with ethical and legal issues as they are likely to arise in a primary care setting? Is there teaching about the use and the effects of psychotropic drugs upon a client's ability to process thoughts and feelings? Is there clear information about the structure of the National Health Service, the relationship between primary and secondary care and possibilities for referral to mental health resources?

The documents in the appendices merit close attention, particularly where they draw a distinction between generic training and training that is specific to working in primary care. Ideally primary care counsellors should have undergone at least four years' training. Three of those years may be on a generic course, as long as it is one that deals in some depth with the issues raised above. But a further year is necessary, either on the original course or as part of it, or through modules taken through continuing professional development, which deals with those aspects that are particular to working in primary care: knowledge of the structure of the NHS, understanding of clinical governance, of multidisciplinary working, of psychotropic medication, of audit, evaluation and research, of legal issues etc.

The document on minimum standards refers to the selection, assessment and supervision of trainees, but how is the prospective student to know whether the standards expected of a course match those of those working in primary care? There are some obvious signs: does the course offer places to anyone, without interview, without preliminary assessment of educational ability and without considering previous work experience. If it does, think again, unless the course is essentially a feeder to a higher-level training, where there are more rigorous selection procedures (perhaps based upon assessment on the preliminary course). Some courses offer pathways into high-level training, but not all provide the opportunities to learn all that is necessary to work in primary care. Unfortunately there are some that appear to pass everyone: unless the initial selection has been rigorous enough to ensure potentially good candidates, such ease of qualification again poses questions. So if the course interviews prospective students, that is a good sign: but a good question to ask at interview is how many students fail to complete the training, often by dropping out because they are not going to make the grade. If the answer is 'none', be warned!

Interviews for places on courses are two-way processes. Just as clients should be able to ask counsellors questions about their training and supervision, or about limits of confidentiality, so prospective students need to ask questions of those who interview them. For example, are all the tutors also practising counsellors? Are those who teach modules in primary care counselling themselves experienced in working in that setting? Questions that address finding placements and supervision, as described below, are also relevant.

I referred above to the different models of counselling that underpin courses, and noted that these models will be largely unfamiliar to the prospective student. The majority of courses describe themselves through their core model, as being person-centred, psychodynamic, cognitive-behavioural, integrative or eclectic – the last expression being largely subsumed currently by the term integrative. The need to work with clients who present different issues, and who demonstrate different abilities to use counselling, suggests that a course that covers many approaches might be most suitable. The older eclectic courses were often of this kind, students sampling each of the major models of working, but mastering none of them. Integrative models have refined this approach, so that there is often a core model that forms the basis upon which a more integrated approach is developed, but where even the core model has begun to utilise elements from different approaches. What seems essential is that in basic training a student is provided with a sufficiently complete model of working – which may be person-centred, may be psychodynamic, may be cognitive-behavioural, existential or a number of other humanistic models. This core model provides a solid base from which to range through other approaches, using the core model to critique them, and using them to critique the core model. It matters little, then, whether the core model is person-centred or some other humanistic approach, psychodynamic, cognitive-behavioural or an integrated model that is more unified than simply being eclectic. That single core model is unlikely to be enough, or even suitable for such a generic group of clients, unless the training branches out to look at the way other models can be drawn upon, and eventually integrated themselves into a counsellor's practice. It follows that a student needs to be wary of any course that teaches a single model (other than 'integrative' as the core model) as if it were the only possible approach. That may be sufficient for some counsellors and therapists in private practice, where clients can be selected; but it is not sufficient for the varied clientele of primary care, or indeed of any other 'public' service.

An essential part of the training of counsellors, psychologists and psychotherapists is based upon practice: practice that is partly achieved on the course itself through skills training; partly through experience of personal therapy for the student herself or himself (that is an essential part of a good training, with a minimum of 40 hours' personal therapy or personal development); and partly through placements and supervision of practice with real clients. There are a large number of courses that do not provide placements, but expect students to find placements. Here is another good aspect to question at interview. Not only is it generally thought undesirable that students should ring round counselling agencies or surgeries asking for a placement; in fact it is very difficult to find placements that way. It might appear obvious, therefore, that the better course to choose is one that has links to placement opportunities, and can match students to placements. A course that has good working relationships with counsellors in primary care may therefore be able to arrange for placements in medical settings – not as a first placement, because this is also generally considered undesirable – once a certain amount of real experience has been gained. Supervision should be provided again either by the course or by the placement, with good working relationships between supervisors and course tutors, so that problems can be ironed out more smoothly, and so that assessment of the placement can be carried out along recognised lines.

Assessing the Competency of Courses as an Employer

Employers have an important part to play in encouraging the development of courses that pay proper attention to counselling in primary care. Where there are local courses where there can be practical liaison between teaching staff and employers, employers have the opportunity to influence the content of modules on primary care counselling; and through the selection of students on placements and through employing graduates of particular courses that meet high standards, employers support those courses, and foster a potential supply of well trained counsellors for themselves.

In addition to the description in the preceding section of the questions that need be asked of counselling courses, which are as valid for employers as they are for prospective students, there are two further ways in which an employer needs to assess the standing of counselling courses: first, in selecting students for placements; second, in appointing new counsellors to the staff, especially where the applicants are more recent graduates and where previous counselling experience can less readily be assessed through references. Chapter Twelve in this volume discusses questions of selection, and the employer is obviously pointed to this for further information.

In the case of selecting counsellors as permanent members of staff, there are more factors than assessment of the merits of the course from which the applicants have graduated. When the employer is appointing a counsellor, the employer will be looking for someone who is confident enough to handle the varied work already described above, as well as someone who maintains good personal and working relationships with other counsellors and with medical and nursing staff; the measure of their competence will only partly be associated with the course(s) they attended, because it will also depend upon self-presentation, obvious expertise in the discussion of case material, previous experience and references, as well as obvious demonstration of the skills and knowledge relevant to primary care. It is possible, especially at the point in the development of specialised training in primary care counselling when a number of experienced counsellors did not have the opportunity of opting for specific training, that some applicants may have trained originally in a weak course, or one that was unable to provide sufficient input on the issues that are particularly relevant to the primary care setting; nevertheless, some of those applicants may have personally and professionally equipped themselves for the primary care counsellor role, through natural ability, through further training and most importantly through previous counselling experience in primary care.

Students on placement are a different matter, although here too it has to be said that even weak courses can have very good students, and good courses can have very weak students, especially at the point where they have as yet engaged in little practice. Nevertheless, what has already been suggested as being the most relevant aspects to look for applies as much to the way in which an employer assesses the merits of a student requesting a placement as to the course he or she is studying. In other words, employers are selecting not just upon the merits of individual students, but also upon the merits of the training they are receiving. This is a further way in which employers can hope to raise standards of competency both in the individual student and in counselling training. In time it is the resulting effects of selection that will count. A sequence of promising placement students from a particular course recommends that course as a source of placement students and of graduates in future, although what has worked in the past does not obviate the necessity of continuing careful selection of applicants and monitoring of courses in future. Conversely, one poor student, even from a respectable course, easily tarnishes the reputation of the course, at least in the short term. It is for that reason that close liaison between course tutors and the employer is a good sign, indicating a level of care and professionalism that suggests worthwhile students.

Conclusion

The explosion of interest in counselling, both in terms of the number of students seeking courses and in terms of employers and institutions seeking to use counsellors, is still relatively recent. Huge steps have been taken by key figures in the leading counselling, psychotherapy and psychology institutions to ensure that this explosion of interest is more controlled, and that responsible standards for training and ongoing practice are set and met. Nevertheless, some of what I have described in this chapter, despite being called 'minimum standards', is still at this point a set of ideals, of guidelines towards which the profession is working. Courses, particularly those set up to cash in on the popularity of counselling, will inevitably take time to implement these measures, if they do at all. It may be that before tighter regulation it is only the market place that will help sort the wheat from the chaff. Even the better courses may not be able yet to fulfil all the requirements listed in the Minimum Training Standards and Personal Specification Protocol for primary care counsellors, although what this author regards as the major requirements of those documents have already been fully met in most of the courses to be recommended.

In other words, as already expressed, choice is in some places limited, and many courses may not yet be able to meet every single recommendation. That does not mean they are bad courses. But if they can provide a solid core training, can develop the necessary blend of caution and confidence that is expected of a good counsellor and can imbue the recognition of the constant need for further training and development, they are what counsellors and therapists often like to call 'good enough'. There are many aspects that make for a good counsellor, of which their initial training is only one element. Attendance on even the best training course can never guarantee that the student will become a good counsellor or therapist; but it certainly helps.

CHAPTER EIGHT

Towards Regulation?

Tim O'Brien

THE first point to establish is that I am not a counsellor and do not work for a counselling organisation; ENTO is a UK-wide independent standards setting body with responsibility for the national occupational standards for counselling, along with a range of other national standards including coaching, mentoring and mediation.

The development of national occupational standards in the UK began with the 1986 White Paper *Working Together – Education and Training*, which proposed that the skills level of the workforce had to increase to ensure effective competitiveness in world markets. The chosen route to achieve this ambition was to develop minimum standards of competence for all occupational sectors and recognise the attainment of the competence through certificated nationally accredited vocational qualifications. The methodology used to determine the national occupational standards was a home grown UK one, which not only involved the assessment of competent performance, but also demanded that the learner had the specific and contextual direct and background knowledge required to be regarded as truly 'competent' and not just an automaton.

A key feature of the development of the national occupational standards has been the involvement of practitioners, employers, professional bodies, awarding bodies, trade unions and national qualifications regulatory bodies. Not only has this been essential to ensure that the national occupational standards are current and relevant, but it has been critical to their adoption and use.

As the national occupational standards describe everyday activities, there has been an increasing use of them as the foundations of a 'licence' to practise, e.g. in the care sector. Equally, some professional bodies use both the national occupational standards and the vocational qualifications as legitimate entry requirements, e.g. health and safety, personnel. This has meant that in some occupational sectors there has been an adjustment of 'professional' standards to synthesise with the 'vocational' standards.

The blurring of the demarcation lines between 'professional' and 'vocational' qualifications, which is part of the government's educational policy, is also reflected in the overlaps between vocational, higher and further education; this is exemplified by the introduction of foundation degrees in England. Taking this further, the qualifications regulatory bodies covering the four UK countries have developed a credit and levelling system to provide a clear comparison and parity ready-reckoner to determine the relationships between vocational and academic qualifications; in England the proposed 'Framework for Achievement' (www.qca.org.uk/10710.html) development is taking the allocation of credits to a very detailed stage.

Although they might seem to have followed a smooth and well planned evolutionary process, the developments have been, as one would expect, erratic and sporadic. There have been territorial conflicts and concerns over dilution of the quality of learning and 'testing' knowledge. There have been changes in government policy that has, since 1986, seen the development of national occupational standards move from lead bodies, to occupational standard councils, to national training organisations and now to sector skills councils. At the same time, the funding bodies have been reorganised and their targets have been changed; the national qualifications regulatory bodies have also changed and taken wider responsibilities. Despite these challenges, the development and use of national occupational standards and vocational qualifications has continued and become part of the training and workforce development language.

Having given some background to the national occupational standards, I must now tackle the question of this chapter: is 'counselling' moving towards regulation? The counselling national occupational standards have now been revised and have widespread support from professionals, representative bodies and trainers. With these national occupational standards, there is the possibility of being able to state, with some precision, that at a particular level of activity, knowledge and professional autonomy a person can be licensed; equally, a person at a lower level of activity cannot be licensed. This can be applied across all areas where 'counselling' is a primary activity. The 'body of knowledge' essential for a professional counsellor is now part of the national occupational standards and can be assessed, as can the ethical environment within which the counsellor has to operate.

What is less certain is the willingness of all counsellors to be regulated and the form such regulation might take; this is perhaps why the newly formed UK Health Professions Council is reluctant to make counselling a regulated profession. The national occupational standards describe the activities involved in counselling and can profile a 'counsellor', but they are not designed to proscribe the profession as a whole or resolve the conflicts between different aspects of counselling or with other professions, such as psychologists. These imperatives must come from practitioners at all levels, who are prepared to be pragmatic and developmental in resolving these disagreements and to seek ways of lowering or removing demarcation barriers.

The development of the national occupational standards involved a steering group (including both of the editors and a number of chapter authors for this book), with members coming from a range of counselling backgrounds with different expectations and demands. It was impressive to see how the group worked flexibly and imaginatively to find common ground without giving up any key principles. It seems that this model of cooperation, where the best interests of the client or user were always paramount, is one that could be used on the wider platform of bringing together colleagues from other related professions, as well as from higher education, to achieve a framework of agreement that could be the foundation of robust but fair regulation.

The building blocks are all available to move towards a regulated profession that has clear entry and progression points. However, is there a need for regulation and, if so, is there a real appetite for a voluntary approach rather than an eventually imposed one? This question has to be answered by practitioners, the profession, representative bodies and, very importantly, employers. If the response is affirmative, the national occupational standards and their relationship to other standards and qualifications will be both useful tools and a template for further work.

The final, and very serious, comment is that the counselling profession in the UK needs to be fully aware of and involved in the national occupational standards programme, because the whole approach to vocational and academic qualifications is increasingly being based on credits and levels. The greater involvement now means a greater influence; reluctance to participate might mean having to work with national occupational and other standards and qualifications that might not be palatable but will be imposed from on high.

Reference

Secretary of State for Employment and Secretary of State for Education and Science (1986) *Working Together – Education and Training*, White Paper. London: HMSO.

CHAPTER NINE

Training Standards for Supervision in Primary Care

Naomi Stewart

Introduction

THE question of training for supervisors of primary care counsellors is surrounded by dilemmas, ambiguities and tensions. These need to considered, understood and addressed. What training do supervisors need to prepare them for the complex set of responsibilities that face them in their role? Who should be undertaking such supervision? There are questions to be addressed about the role, remit and accountability of supervisors. Add to this the unique setting of primary care with its fast-paced organisational culture and the fact that counsellors are drawn from a variety of trainings, each with a particular set of values and principles informing the way they practise, and it gives a picture of the complexity of the supervisory task. The growth of counselling in primary care needs to be supported by well trained and competent supervisors. At present there is no formal requirement for supervisors to be trained and accredited, although accrediting bodies like the British Association of Counselling and Psychotherapy (BACP) and Counsellors in Primary Care (CPC) have processes whereby supervisors can be accredited. The United Kingdom Council for Psychotherapy (UKCP) and British Psychoanalytic Council (BCP) do not currently register supervisors. The British Association of Psychoanalytic and Psychodynamic Supervisors (BAPPS) accredits supervisors who have undertaken an approved training or have served a long apprenticeship as a supervisor. There is no agreed requirement within the profession that practitioners supervising trainees or trained counsellors have to have qualifications as a supervisor or indeed what constitutes a good supervision training. There is a pressing need for agreed basic training standards that can apply across the profession of supervision with core curriculum and learning outcomes.

Although therapy and supervision are firmly linked together in most practitioners' minds, the question of what makes a good supervisor is rather more problematic. For many years an apprenticeship model prevailed. Assumptions were made that good therapists would naturally become good supervisors. Senior members of a profession usually undertake supervision, which suggests that maturity, experience, knowledge and skill are required of the supervisor. For many supervisors the transition from therapist to supervisor was made when either they or their organisation considered that they had sufficient experience to supervise. Rather like becoming a new parent, the therapist relied on his or her internalised experiences to develop a supervisory style and identity. Consequently, many supervisors learned their craft in the crucible of experience.

The recognition that supervision is a distinct activity led to the growth of supervisory trainings, each with its own view of the generic skills required of a supervisor, course content and training requirements. Some, but by no means all, include understanding of the organisational setting. However, as Lawson (2000) outlines, 'many outside the profession, and indeed within it, may be surprised to learn that a supervisor who has successfully completed a reputable supervision training course may have undertaken less than 20 hours of supervision in order to obtain their qualification'. Supervision is a hugely complex activity and even generic skills should not be considered basic but need to be viewed as a sophisticated set of capacities and competencies that need to be developed. I suggest that the basic entry criteria for counsellors wishing to train as supervisors should be substantial clinical experience in the area of counselling, preferably in primary care or a similar NHS setting for at least three years. Furthermore, therapists making the transition from counsellor to supervisor should undertake training that is concurrent with this transition. Supervision trainings offer an opportunity to think about the different challenges and tensions within the supervisory relationship and therefore facilitate the development of professional practice and identity as a supervisor. There need to be agreed routes to being registered as a supervisor, with accredited courses, a required number of post-qualification supervision hours and clearly laid out equivalents for experienced supervisors. Supervision needs to be supervised and subject to a set of ethics and guidelines, and supervisors should be subject to identified complaints procedures. As the profession moves towards statutory regulation there will be greater demands to ensure adequately trained and competent supervisors.

Important questions to consider are as follows. What are the essential ingredients of a good supervisor? Or, in other words, what are the generic competencies required to supervise? What purpose and function does supervision fulfil? Then, what are the particular requirements needed of a supervisor working within primary care? Who are best placed to undertake such supervision and what kind of training do they need to prepare them for their role? My own view is that any supervisor practising within the primary care setting needs to have substantial clinical experience, good generic supervisory competencies, substantial supervised supervision hours and further specialist skills in relation to the complex and demanding organisational setting of primary care. It is essential that supervisors have a knowledge and skills framework that informs their practice. I will outline the complexity of the supervisory task and link this to the generic and specialist skills required of primary care supervisors. Generic skills constellate around understanding of the supervisory task and the process of supervision and can be grouped together as supervisory capacities:

The supervisory capacities

- The person specification: qualities of the good supervisor.
- Creating a supervisory space.
- The supervisory task.
- Supervisory difficulties and anxieties.
- The dynamics of the supervisory process.
- A sound working knowledge of the ethical and legal framework, with clarity about the supervisor's role in relation to the patient, the supervisee and the organisation.

Specialist knowledge and skills

- The impact of the setting, organisational dynamics and defences.
- Relational dynamics: the challenge of multiprofessional working.
- The demands of the work in the primary care setting.
- Assessment skills with an internalised developmental framework that facilitates understanding and recognition of different psychopathology, managing and containing risk.

These skills would, of course, be underpinned by minimum standards of counselling practice concerning working respectfully with issues of difference and diversity, an internalised working model of human development, including theories of thinking and the mind, gendered and culturally influenced ways of understanding the self and an understanding of change and how this may be encouraged.

The Person Specification: Qualities of a Good Supervisor

Although there is little research evidence demonstrating the effectiveness of supervision, many would agree that good supervision offers a vital space for reflection and containment, greatly enhancing understanding of the work, further learning and continuing professional development. What do we look for from a supervisor? The supervisee looks for a person of good standing in the profession, someone who has greater experience and a sound knowledge base and who demonstrates a capacity for empathy, attunement and creative thinking. Practitioners are looking for a safe environment in which they can feel respected and valued so that they feel able to share their work with all the attendant uncertainties, struggles and joys. The supervisee needs the supervisor to be reliably and responsively available in order to feel held and contained in the work and the supervisor needs the supervisee to be open, honest and willing to engage in the process of supervision. The supervisory environment may be either individual or group but they are distinct processes and supervisors should have had training in both models. Fundamentally, the supervisor needs to have a capacity to understand and contain the process of the therapeutic relationship and to be able to facilitate the learning and development of the supervisee. According to Rock:

> The good supervisors seem to invite their supervisees to identify with them, to take them as their mentors, and to encourage autonomy. They demonstrate to the supervisees how to appreciate and use their responses to the ambiguous and anxiety-provoking task of conducting psychotherapy. The learning is fostered by a relationship that is experienced by the supervisee as reciprocal, mutual and trusting. (Rock, 1997)

A mutual and trusting relationship requires an appreciation of diversity and difference, and supervisors need to be sensitive to issues of inequality and discrimination, recognising the talents and limitations of the supervisee. Driver speaks of the development of supervisory authority, which derives from balancing the different foci of 'the needs and clinical issues of the patient, the learning needs of the supervisee, and the impact and limitations of the institution in which supervision takes place' (Driver, 2002).

Creating a Supervisory Space: A Facilitating Environment

Establishing the frame of the supervision is essential in the provision of the right kind of space in which to engage in the supervisory process. The supervisor's skill and capacity in developing what Winnicott (1963) has termed a 'facilitating environment' is a fundamental cornerstone of supervision. The supervisor needs to be able to create a safe space in which it is possible to bring the work and to feel safely held and free to play with ideas. Supervision contracts provide a useful way of establishing the frame of supervision, making clear the expectations and requirements of the relationship. 'At the heart of Winnicott's concept of the facilitating environment is the good enough mother who is sensitive and attuned to her baby's needs, and where there is a sense of a good "fit" between baby's anticipation and mother's provision' (M. Thomas, 2005). We know that play is more likely to happen freely from within the context of a secure attachment (Bowlby, 1988; Driver, 2005a). The supervisor needs to work actively to create the kind of space in which it is possible to raise mistakes, difficulties and troubling feelings towards patients and, at times, the supervisor. The therapeutic concepts of attunement, intersubjectivity, reverie, containment, thinking and linking, free-association and imagination are at the heart of the supervisory experience. A capacity for empathy, identification and reflective functioning, and a willingness to take inside the therapist/patient couple, is a prerequisite for the work of both therapy and supervision (Fonagy and Target, 1998; Astor, 2000, 2003). Bion's theory of thinking and concepts of container/contained are fundamental here (Bion, 1962a, b). Reisenberg-Malcolm (2001) describes containment as a process of mental digestion. These ideas generate the conditions for the reflective thinking that is essential for digesting and therefore containing the work. This is particularly important for supervision in the primary care context, where there is little time to think and digest experience.

The Supervisory Task

One of the main functions of supervision is to ensure the best possible psychotherapy practice. The supervisor's function comprises containment and support, an educative and mentoring role and identifying with the different positions of client, therapist, organisation and supervisor. According to Driver, 'Being a supervisor and supervising the work of others requires the development of an array of skills, including the ability to discover, understand, translate and interpret unconscious processes and inter-relational dynamics and apply this understanding within the supervisory relationship' (Driver, 2005b, p. xvii). The supervisory task is to help the therapist to grasp hold of these dynamics as they unfold in the work and in supervision. This involves supervisor and supervisee thinking together about the work in a similar way to the parental couple thinking about the child. The supervisor helps the counsellor to enable clients to find words to express what they have always known but have not been able to express (Martin, 2005). Mollon (1997), Stewart (2002) and Crawford (2005) highlight the essence of the thinking process, which is linked to the right hemisphere of the brain involved with free association, the imaginal world and phantasy responses. The nature of the supervisory task inevitably makes for reverie, mindfulness and reflection, rather than resolving, advising and solving. The busy setting of primary care, with its high through-put of patients, seriously challenges reflective thinking and may impel both counsellor and supervisor to premature action. The supervisor in primary care is constantly challenged to hold a thinking space that Keats (1817) describes as a *negative capability*, 'of being in uncertainties, mystery, doubts, without any irritable reaching after facts and reason'. This capacity has to be held in creative tension with the supervisor's need to know and role in assessing the supervisee's practice.

Supervisory Difficulties and Anxieties

The anxieties aroused in the supervisee by both the work of therapy and then bringing this work to the supervisor has been well documented (Zinkin, 1995; Lidmila, 1997; Mollon, 1997; Knight, 2003). The supervisory process may stimulate anxieties and shame in both the supervisee and supervisor around being 'good enough'. Creating the necessary facilitating environment from which the supervisee can feel safe enough to bring his or her work is not straightforward, but particularly so when there is a 'negative supervisory reaction' (Lane, 1990; Thomas, 2005). At times it is not possible to create a safe space where the supervisory couple can play together. Lidmila highlights the importance of reaching a position in supervision where 'innocence and ignorance become revealed, and curiosity and desire may be safely experienced' (Lidmila, 1997, p. 37). This can only happen if the supervisor clearly holds in mind the distinction and boundary between supervision and therapy. Fordham (1961) emphasises the importance of treating supervisees as colleagues, not patients. This is an important distinction to hold on to because it can be easy to stray into the area of therapy, which is inappropriate in the supervisory relationship. This can be a particularly challenging boundary to hold firm when difficulties arise in the supervisory relationship or there are difficulties in establishing a supervisory alliance. The transition from counsellor to supervisor is not always an easy one and particularly so when difficulties crystallise between the supervisory couple. The supervisor may feel unprepared for such difficulties and deskilled, stripped of his or her usual interpretive approach. Supervision training offers the novice supervisor the opportunity to understand that such difficulties are not unusual and to have confidence in his or her approach and capacity to weather the storm.

Undertaking a training in supervision can help supervisors to develop awareness of their own personal supervisory styles and to be aware of their strengths and limitations. This awareness needs to develop through a supervisory relationship in which supervision practice can be supervised. The urge to be active in theorising, formulating, understanding and directing are all potential supervisory pitfalls that arise in relation to anxieties stimulated by the nature of the work. This is a particular difficulty aroused by the busy, 'doing to' culture of primary care (Wolff, 1971). This also requires that the supervisor understands the seductive charms of position, power and knowledge that is inherent in the supervisory role without recourse to showing off or restricting the supervisees' autonomy, requiring them to conform to the supervisor's own style of working. Perry's essential supervisory qualities include 'Robust debtate, a sense of humour, appropriate humility, imaginative leaps, and the sharing of relevant theory and experience' (Perry, 2003, p. 205). Casement (1997, p. 267) suggests that the supervisor is seeking to facilitate the development of an internalised supervisor. In order to do this, the supervisor needs to be able to value and encourage the supervisee's own style of working and approach to the work. Although the supervisor may share associations and reactions to the supervisee's material, the task is not to impose or direct. Eigen (1997) cautions against 'being too good'. This requires that supervisors be aware of any unresolved narcissistic needs to be admired and have a capacity to recognise envy, rivalry and competition in both themselves and their supervisees.

The supervisor also has the difficult task of working with an absent patient that has to be grasped through imagination and countertransference responses (Zinkin, 1995; Martin, 2002). The dynamics of patient, counsellor and the supervisor's own responses have to be recognised, reflected upon and made sense of. Power dynamics, envy, rivalry, jealousy and narcissistic gratifications can powerfully emerge in the supervisor, who then has the task of understanding their source and acting appropriately. An analytic attitude is crucial here and Mander refers to this objectivity as a selflessness, of not using supervision to gratify one's narcissistic needs for possession and admiration. 'It is an ability to be inside and outside simultaneously, of participating and observing, at one remove from the therapeutic couple and yet being involved as a participant in the supervisory relationship' (Mander, 1998, p. 59).

The Dynamics of the Supervisory Process

The strength of the unconscious processes that are at the centre of therapeutic work are powerfully recreated in the therapy and in the supervision. Pickvance (1997, p. 139) asserts that effective supervision demands that the supervisor has an awareness of how these dynamics may help or inhibit the supervisory task. According to Driver (2005a, p. xvii), 'The aim of interpretation within supervision is to engage the supervisee's internal world and stimulate dialogue between the conscious and unconscious in an internal dialectic that generates insight.' At the centre of a supervisory knowledge and skills framework is an understanding that the dynamics of the relationship between the therapist and patient emerge in the relationship between therapist and supervisor in what is called parallel process (Mattinson, 1975; Bromberg, 1982). Coming from a psychoanalytic training, I maintain that the use of both the counsellor's and supervisor's countertransference responses is a particularly useful way into understanding the patient and what is happening in the therapeutic relationship. (Winnicott, 1949, 1960; Searles, 1979; Berman, 2000). Mattinson

(1975) emphasises the importance of distance and difference in the supervisory role, which requires a capacity for both being pulled in and then separating again. Understanding of the dynamics that emerge within the triangular three person nature of the supervisory relationship is fundamental to the skills and approach of the supervisor. Add to the mix the therapist's and supervisor's own internal worlds and countertransference responses coupled with organisational dynamics and it gives a flavour of the complexity of the supervisory arena.

The fact that the supervisor is closest to understanding what is happening between counsellor and client in the privacy of the therapy means that the supervisor has to provide an environment in which supervisees feel sufficiently safe to share their work in an honest and open way without fear of judgement or shame. Barden (2001, p. 46) writes: 'But for the counselled public, the supervisor remains the only person besides the client who is likely to have any consistent or detailed awareness of what goes on inside the counselling room.' The supervisor needs to be able to hold together the tension of creating an environment in which it is safe for supervisees to be themselves and to play without splitting off or resisting their role in monitoring the quality and safety of the work.

The Ethical and Legal Framework: Tensions around the Supervisor's Responsibility and Accountability

Confusions remain around the nature and purpose of supervision, standards of competency and the extent and limits of the supervisor's responsibility and remit (King and Wheeler, 1998, 1999; Bower et al., 2001). King (2001) surveyed counselling supervisors' understanding of their clinical responsibility in relation to the work of their supervisees. Wheeler and King (2001, p. 3) reported that the results were 'both surprising and worrying, as they revealed that there was considerable confusion about the nature and extent of responsibility that supervisors take for the work of their supervisees'. This understanding is essential for any supervisor but is complicated by the ambiguity and tensions within the supervisory role. King and Wheeler's research points to significant anxieties in supervisors concerning potential supervisory difficulties and damage to their reputation. The experienced supervisors surveyed were 'without exception' selective about the counsellors they accepted for supervision in order to 'minimise risk and uncertainty' and to avoid taking on inexperienced or unknown counsellors. Counselling supervisors were also reluctant to take action when they had serious concerns about their supervisee's work (King and Wheeler, 1998, p. 307). Furthermore, responsibility and decisions about which patients to bring for supervision lay with the supervisee, not with the supervisor, which can be problematic when there are concerns about poor practice. Burton et al.'s (1998) survey of counsellors' experiences of supervision identified that supervisees felt less satisfied with the supervisor when difficulties in the work or the supervisory relationship were explored by the supervisor. Both King and Wheeler's and Burton et al.'s research highlight the anxieties around supervision and the confusion surrounding the supervisor's responsibilities and accountability. Barden helps us to understand that this confusion is exacerbated by the supervisor's need to split off the duality that exists within the supervisory role and that an essential capacity is to be able to tolerate and hold the tensions in an integrated way. The accountability aspect of supervision, with its attendant need for judgements of the counsellor's work, seems to be problematic for many supervisors and may represent the shadow side of supervision, hidden behind a more acceptable developmental aspect. Barden writes about this in relation to the BAC Code of Ethics and Practice.

> The codes struggle with this apparent contradiction, creating an uneven duality that makes it hard for the supervisor and the counsellor to know precisely how to tread the line between the

> demands of monitoring and of support. Terms such as 'monitor', 'ensure', 'develop', 'encourage', 'maintain', 'enhance', 'support' and 'challenge' are used in the code in relation to the supervisor's role. A supervisor must hold the capacity to do all of these things; this is only possible if one can find a way to stop holding them in opposition to each other and to seek a pluralistic approach that allows the co-existence of such apparent opposites. . . . It may be that the question is not whether supervision is primarily about either support or monitoring, but whether it could truly be one without the other. (Barden, 2001, p. 46)

Henderson (2001, p. 93) draws attention to the shared care approach in primary care and notes that the GP does not refer a patient for counselling but retains responsibility for the care of the patient. This is something akin to delegation. Jones (1989) suggests that supervision is the means by which institutions and agencies ensure standards of practice and protect themselves against allegations of malpractice. However, this position is not without complications because the supervisor's view of the counselling work is based on the supervisee's account rather than on direct observation, placing the supervisor in a difficult and anomalous position. None the less, the supervisor is the only person who gets remotely close to understanding the quality of the work with the patient.

A case that is often quoted is that of Anthony Smith (Southern Derbyshire Health Authority, 1996), who killed his mother and half-brother while being seen by a counsellor in a primary care setting. The report of the inquiry into his care raises questions about the training and competence of both the counsellor and the supervisor.

> The question is raised as to why nothing happened with regard to the psychotic symptoms during the year of counselling. This was because they were not detected by the counsellor. This suggests that the training of counsellors does not provide them with the necessary skills to allow them to recognise serious psychotic symptoms in their clients. (SDHA, 1996, p. 34)

The Report goes on to address the question of supervision and the need for adequate systems of supervision to be in place. However, King and Wheeler's (1998) research demonstrates that many patients are never taken to supervision and this raises debates about whether this is possible or even desirable. There is no agreed understanding of the nature of the supervisory relationship and no clear resolution of the dilemmas around supervisory responsibility. Zinkin (1995) argues that there is a problem with the word supervisee because it suggests that the focus of supervision is the supervisee rather than the patient. However, the BAC (1996) supervisor's code of ethics stresses that the supervisor should be looking after the interests of the client. Supervisory dilemmas often constellate around such tensions and supervisors are regularly faced with conflicts of interest around client/supervisee/confidentiality/competing risks, all of which have to be balanced and held together in an often uneasy tension. Dilemmas often appear around confidentiality because the supervisor has bear in mind the confidentiality of both the client and supervisee.

Many counselling courses include training on ethics but offer little or no training on the law (Gibson and Pope, 1993). The BACP stresses that counsellors should 'take all reasonable steps to be aware of current law as it applies to their counselling practice' (BAC, 1997, p. B.1.6.1). Both counselling and supervision trainings would do well to emulate social work trainings, which do include training on law. Jenkins (2001) clarifies that:

> supervision could be seen at various times to relate to one or more of the following:
>
> - *clinical responsibility* for the delegated care of a client, as in a medical model of patient care
> - *professional responsibility* for the overall quality of decision making regarding a client
> - *accountability* in line management terms for decision making, under terms and conditions of employment

- *individual legal liability* for the process or outcomes of client care
- *vicarious liability* as the employee of the organisation responsible for client care.

Jenkins (2001) maintains that supervisors need to understand the legal liabilities attached to their role and that these are influenced by the context in which supervisors practise. This is particularly apposite because our society is steadily moving towards an increasingly litigious culture. Litton (2001, p. 1) considers the prevailing mood to be one of 'why just complain, when you can claim?' The supervisor is often required to contain both the counsellor's and his or her own fear of failure and fantasies around being publicly pilloried and shamed. Such worries and the reality of working within a blame culture may make it even harder to retain a capacity to think. The primary care supervisor really does need to afford a central role to the provision of a reflective space. This is further complicated by the organisational culture geared towards processing large numbers of patients because this does not lend itself to reflection and thinking. Given that primary care is a busy, fast-paced service characterised by a diverse range of difficulties that need to be identified, assessed and treated within a short space of time, the counsellor's and supervisor's capacities to manage risk need to be finely tuned. The combination of pressures that have to be faced may drive both the counsellor and supervisor into an unthinking position in which the safety of the supervisory couple takes precedence over the needs of the patient. Responsibility for transparency and accountability are important components of the practice of supervision. Ethical and legal tensions are a troubling and increasingly frequent aspect of any counsellor's and supervisor's work. These tensions draw our attention to debates around frequency of supervision and whether all work should be subject to supervision. King and Wheeler offer two different responses to the research findings. King questions the effectiveness of supervision and argues for greater accountability, regulation and clarity within the BACP codes of ethics. Wheeler argues against a 'rule-bound' approach, preferring informed practice, with Codes of Ethics providing helpful guidelines. 'It is not possible to legislate in a way that takes account of all the nuances of a situation.' Legal and ethical dilemmas are not easily resolved but many counsellors and supervisors seem to be unaware of these issues, leaving them vulnerable when difficulties arise. Wheeler and King's important work really highlights the need for supervisors to be adequately trained and competent to practise. I suggest that central to this is the development of robust understanding of the legal and ethical tensions contained within the supervisory role.

Organisational Dynamics: The Setting and Work of Primary Care

The organisational context for the work will always impact on the nature of therapy and therefore on supervision (Wiener and Sher, 1988; Shane and Shane, 1995; Berman, 2000; Dammers and Wiener, 2002; Stewart, 2002, 2004). The primary care setting is a particularly good example of this, with its fast-paced culture of 'busyness', multiprofessional working and time-limited work. Counsellors working in primary care are faced with the challenging task of rapid through-put of patients, assessing patients and delivering psychological therapies in a fast-paced, frenetic culture. This creates a working atmosphere that Zabarfi (2000, p. 100) has described as one of 'tangible urgency', a world away from the quiet, comfortable environment that is often taught as an essential ingredient of the therapeutic frame. Many counsellors in supervision share their feelings of being overwhelmed by the sheer volume of patient numbers and the intensity of pain and loss that they are expected to manage and contain. Counsellors are constantly working with rapid assessment, beginnings and endings, which is demanding and tiring. The supervisor is essential in helping the supervisee engage with these painful aspects of work without becoming emotionally anaesthetised, overly defended or simply overwhelmed by the enormity of the process. The pressures of the setting are inevitably recreated within supervision and the supervisor needs to be able to grasp the significance of these and how they impact on the work with the patient and supervisor. This fast-paced approach to the work is often recreated in supervision through parallel process so that the counsellor may bring many patients in little depth, challenging both the counsellor's and supervisor's capacity to take in and reflect on the work. Hinshelwood and Skogstad (2002, p. 123) suggest that specific settings promote particular defences and that within primary care a manic defence predominates because the work frequently involves suffering related to loss, illness, dying and death. Knowledge of organisational dynamics and defences harnessed with a good understanding of the demands of the work on the counsellor and the difficulties involved in multiprofessional working are essential for the primary care supervisor.

Relational Dynamics and Supervision

In other counselling settings, the patient may have an exclusive relationship with the therapist and contact with other professions is kept separate from the counselling relationship. In primary care, however, there is multiprofessional involvement, adding to the complexity of relationships, with even greater potential for professional tensions and splitting. Supervisors have an invaluable part to play in reflecting upon relationships that coexist in the primary care setting. The three-person, oedipal nature of relationships within primary care has been identified and highlighted. and this can emerge as GP/counsellor/patient and patient/counsellor/supervisor matrices (Jones et al., 1994; Hopkins and O'Callaghan, 1999). Jones et al. (1994, pp. 545–6) stress the complexity of potential transference relationships and the oedipal dimensions that arise in primary care, with its approach of shared care. The triangular nature of the supervisory relationship has been much stressed, with dynamics of inclusion and exclusion (Mattinson, 1975).

Hopkins and O'Callaghan (1999, p. 42) make the important point that many of the complications are unseen and this suggests that they may be unconsciously driven. Eatock and Bond (2002, p. 172) stress the complexity of the interaction between the web of relationships within the primary care team and the relationship difficulties of the patient: 'Poor personal relationships can fracture the delivery of service, induce high levels of stress and ultimately lead to the collapse of services or the practice itself. The quality of relationships between colleagues has an impact on the relationships between staff and patients.'

The supervisor is best placed to stand outside the heat and tension of these relational dynamics and to enable the counsellor to see just where unconscious factors are coming into play. The supervisor may be able to hold together the tensions involved in splitting and projective identification and help the counsellor to communicate with involved members of the primary care team to facilitate good therapeutic work. This serves to protect as much as is possible against the counsellor or other members of the primary care team acting out the patient's difficulties in relation to each other. This can be likened to the support that the wider family gives to a mother caring for a young baby. The supervisor may need to take an active part in enabling the counsellor to become a valued part of the primary care team. This is essential if the therapist is to feel held and supported by their working environment. My own experience of supervising primary care counsellors has frequently focused on patients' attempts to externalise their own dynamics through splitting, which then emerged in the primary care team in a destructive and disintegrating way. Supervisors have a particularly vital role to play in helping involved professionals to come together as a healthy parental couple to discuss issues relating to the patient. The supervisor will model the process of coming together with the counsellor as a healthy parental couple who can think about the patient, tolerate anxiety and bear disagreements in order that good therapeutic work can take place.

The Particular Demands of Work in the Primary Care Setting

Working in primary care involves seeing high numbers of patients, often seeing many distressed people in rapid succession. According to Wiener and Sher (1988, p. 75), 'There may be strong conscious or unconscious pressure to adopt a work-style like that of the GPs, with a fast through-put of patients seen for short periods of time, and to take on "impossible patients".' This fast-paced culture regularly emerges in supervision, as greater numbers of patients need to be thought about than is the case in other therapeutic settings. It is not just the sheer volume of patient work but also that the counsellor has to manage what Lees (1997, p. 36) called the 'bottomless pit of suffering' involved in the work. The impact of this suffering may feel overwhelming and therefore can be difficult to stay with and may be defended against. This can make it difficult for the counsellor to engage with the suffering in a way that is helpful to the patient. Regular supervision is essential in enabling the counsellor to remain emotionally available to the patient and to understand the difficulties and struggles in doing this. In my own experience, being on site and available as a supervisor is important because difficulties and dilemmas may not wait for a monthly supervision slot!

Primary care work poses a further challenge to supervisors in that counsellors employed in this setting come from a range of theoretical orientations, such as psychodynamic, person-centred, transactional analysis, gestalt and CBT. This requires the primary care supervisor to have a familiarity with and understanding of these different approaches. While supervisors may have their own model of practice they cannot afford to be exclusively partisan when approaching the task of supervision. Supervisors need to be able to respect and work with the diverse range of approaches to counselling.

Assessment Skills

Much of primary care work is time-limited, requiring supervisors to have had substantial experience of this approach. Good assessment skills are crucial in the selection of patients for counselling. Very often assessment is only a small part of a counsellor's training yet the counsellor is expected to undertake complex assessments of a patient's suitability and capacity to work within a time-limited frame. Assessment involves developing a therapeutic alliance, getting a sense of patients' difficulties in their past and present relationships, identifying unconscious patterns, undertaking a risk assessment if necessary and gaining a sense of what each particular patient needs. Although the counsellor could potentially work with the supervisor around patient selection and formulation of the dynamic focus, the fast throughput of patients may make this impossible to achieve.

Counsellors and supervisors need specialist training in assessment to develop a sound knowledge base, which should include theories of development, including theories of thinking and the mind and psychopathology. There needs to be 'conceptualisation and understanding of how the person to be treated came to be in need of treatment in the first place' (Cook and Buirski, 1990, p. 78). This knowledge base is particularly important in relation to work undertaken with disturbed and disturbing patients. This need was highlighted in the Anthony Smith case mentioned earlier, where the counsellor did not have the necessary training to recognise a psychotic episode. Having competence in assessing suitability for counselling is foundational for both counsellor and supervisor. This involves having a sound understanding of risk assessment. Hickey's (2005) study identifies the lack of adequate training and practice in this important area. The results show that there is an urgent need for training in risk assessment. Often such training takes the form of a one-day CPD course that may go some way to addressing the lack of competence but is simply not adequate to equip counsellors and supervisors to engage in a competent way with risk assessment. Add to this Bower et al.'s (2001) findings around lack of competence with regard to role definition, clinical governance, appropriate qualification and training and it becomes clear just how essential it is that supervisors are competent in risk assessment. This is a sophisticated area that presents the supervisor with difficult and troubling dilemmas that often require complex multiple judgements of competing risks and a capacity to contain anxiety around these. Many of these dilemmas cannot be resolved but need to be openly thought about, considered, contained and recorded. Without an understanding of the structure and working of the NHS and where the primary care counsellor fits into the picture, risk assessment skills are going to be severely limited. Hickey (2005, p. 9) asserts: 'The lack of training means that practitioners do not keep up to date with issues such as maintaining an awareness of high-risk groups, gaining knowledge and skills related to guidelines, protocols and record keeping, and the value of adopting risk-related measuring and scoring systems and tools.'

Such studies are worrying but do confirm the experience of both counsellors and supervisors working in primary care. Time and again counsellors have said that their training did not sufficiently prepare them for the complexity of their work. Given that the current generation of primary care counsellors may well be the supervisors of the future, there is an urgent need for post-graduation training specifically for counsellors intending to practise in primary care. This point goes hand in hand with the need for supervision trainings that can specialise in primary care. This could take the form of either a primary care module or preferably specifically designed training for those intending to practise within primary care. It is simply crucial that supervisors are drawn from those who are the most experienced and competent within their profession. Certainly a counsellor should have at least six years' experience of counselling within primary care before contemplating supervision training. I agree with Wheeler's assertion:

> Supervision is a highly skilled and responsible task that must be reserved for the most experienced counsellors. It should not be seen as a natural and automatic progression from counsellor training. Not all counsellors will be suited to being supervisors and most should wait until they have substantial clinical experience before embarking on such training. (Wheeler, 2000, pp. 334–5)

My own view is that supervision is an ongoing requirement of the work rather than an activity that needs to be concentrated in the early stages of a counsellor's professional development. This is because the work of counselling is always subject to blindspots and acting out and especially so when working with patients who are distressed and disturbed. Primary care counsellors do not undertake the easiest work as is often supposed, and even the most experienced counsellor needs to have the support, safety and protection that is afforded both the client and counsellor through the work of supervision. I would like to add a final word about supervision of supervision. Supervisors also need to be able to take their work for supervision. Mander (2002) presents a balanced picture of this area and cautions against an unwieldy hierarchy. 'Sailing between the Scylla of authoritarianism and the Charybdis of permissiveness is the dangerous and difficult craft of supervision, and the supervisor's supervisor has the responsible task of ensuring a safe passage, of navigating the inexperienced and when the worst comes to the worst, of rescuing the shipwrecked' (Mander, 2002, p. 134).

Conclusion

In this chapter, I have highlighted the complexities of the supervisory role in relation to some of the supervisory skills and capacities that are involved. I have sought to demonstrate just how challenging a task it is to offer good supervisory practice and that generic supervisory skills are by no means basic. I maintain that the minimum entry requirements for generic supervision training should be substantial clinical experience as a counsellor within primary care or an equivalent NHS setting. Consequently, I take the view that supervision is an ongoing requirement of the work rather than an activity that needs to be concentrated in the early stages of a counsellor's professional development. I have suggested that counsellors making the transition to supervisor should undertake a supervision training that is concurrent with this transition. This facilitates the development of professional identity as a supervisor. Supervisors would then work towards accreditation by building up their supervision hours. This supervision should be supervised by an experienced supervisor.

Working in the primary care setting is not, as is often supposed, the softer end of counselling work. Primary care counselling is a complex and challenging area for any counsellor to engage with. Furthermore, the organisational setting of primary care confers a particular set of difficulties that impact on the work of the counsellor. These need to be recognised, thought about and understood. This complexity necessitates that supervisors working in this demanding environment should have additional specialist training. Primary care is a unique setting characterised by a distinctive culture and multiprofessional working. My own view is that specific supervision trainings need to be developed that offer advanced and specialist training in primary care. This is the best possible way to ensure the development of adequately trained and competent supervisors qualified to work in the sophisticated and demanding environment of primary care.

This is an interesting time in our profession's history, with an increasing emphasis on the professionalisation of psychotherapy and counselling and the DoH movement towards statutory regulation in 2008. Statutory regulation may well have an impact on the practice of supervision, making it a formal requirement of the profession and linking it more closely to clinical governance, accountability and responsibility. The report on Harold Shipman has yet to be published, but the 2005 UKCP AGM keynote speech emphasised that post-Shipman there may be greater clinical accountability for supervisors with recommendations for appropriately trained and competent supervisors (Wake, 2005). It is essential that the profession is able to demonstrate clearly what formal requirements there are for putting supervisors in place. Organisations that employ counsellors and supervisors need to be transparent about what criteria they are using for the selection of their supervisors. Each organisation needs to have a developed framework that ensures high standards of clinical and supervisory governance to ensure the delivery of high-quality counselling services in the primary care setting. All supervisors need to have developed a supervisory rationale that they can formulate and articulate. This rationale should include a particular understanding of their tasks as supervisors and clarity about the nature of their role and responsibilities in relation to the patient, supervisee, organisation and the law.

Acknowledgements

Deep appreciation and gratitude goes to my supervisor for teaching me what it means to be a good supervisor and for providing a containing space in which to think about the work. Further, profound thanks go to my supervisees who share their work with me.

References

Astor, J. (2000) Some reflections on empathy and reciprocity in the use of countertransference between supervisor and supervisee. *Journal of Analytical Psychology*, 45, 367–83.

Astor, J. (2003) Empathy in the use of countertransference between supervisor and supervisee. In J. Wiener, R. Mizen and J. Duckham (eds), *Supervising and Being Supervised. A Practice in Search of a Theory*. Basingstoke: Palgrave Macmillan.

BAC (1996) *The Code of Ethics and Practice for Supervisors of Counsellors*. Rugby: BAC.

BAC (1997) *The Code of Ethics and Practice for Counsellors*. Rugby: BAC.

Barden, N. (2001) The responsibility of the supervisor in the British Association for Counselling and Psychotherapy's Codes of Ethics and Practice. In S. Wheeler and D. King (eds), *Supervising Counsellors. Issues of Responsibility*. London: Sage.

Berman, E. (2000) Psychoanalytic supervision: the intersubjective development. *International Journal of Psychoanalysis*, 81, 273–90.

Bion, W. R. (1962a) A theory of thinking. *International Journal of Psycho-Analysis*, 43, 306–10.

Bion, W. R. (1962b) *Learning from Experience*. London: Heinemann.

Bower, P., Foster, J. and Mellor-Clark, J. (2001) *Quality in Counselling in Primary Care: A Guide for Effective Commissioning and Clinical Governance*. London: National Research and Development Centre.

Bowlby, J. (1988) *A Secure Base: Clinical Applications of Attachment Theory*. London: Routledge.

Bromberg, P. (1982) The supervisory process and parallel process in psychoanalysis. *Contemporary Psychoanalysis*, 18(1), 92–111.

Burton, M., Henderson, P. and Curtis Jenkins, G. (1998) Primary care counsellors' experience of supervision. *Counselling*, 9(2), 122–33.

Butterton, M. and Murphy, A. (2002) The search for a new model of clinical supervision in a primary care practice setting. In J. Foster and A. Murphy (eds), *Supervision of Psychological Therapists Working in Primary Care*. Bognor Regis: CPC.

Casement, P. (1997) Towards autonomy: some thoughts on psychoanalytic supervision. In M. Rock (ed.), *Psychodynamic Supervision. Perspectives of the Supervisor and the Supervisee*. New Jersey: Jason Aronson Inc.

Cook, H. and Buirski, P. (1990) Countertransference in psychoanalytic supervision: an heuristic model. *Psychoanalysis and Psychotherapy*, 8(1), 77–87.

Crawford, S. (2005) Free association and supervision. In C. Driver and E. Martin (eds), *Supervision and the Analytic Attitude*. London: Whurr.

Dammers, J. and Wiener, J. (2002) Developing a role for counselling in the primary health care team. In J. Keithley, T. Bond and G. Marsh (eds), *Counselling in Primary Care*, 2nd edn. Oxford: Oxford University Press.

Driver, C. (2002) Introduction: orientation and themes. In C. Driver and E. Martin (eds), *Supervising Psychotherapy*. London: Sage.

Driver, C. (2005a) Introduction. Supervision: the interface of theory and practice. In C. Driver and E. Martin (eds), *Supervision and the Analytic Attitude*. London: Whurr.

Driver, C. (2005b) Attachment and the supervisory alliance. In C. Driver and E. Martin (eds), *Supervision and the Analytic Attitude*. London: Whurr.

Eatock, J. and Bond, T. (2002) Problems of interpersonal relationships. In J. Keithley, T. Bond and G. Marsh (eds), *Counselling in Primary Care*, 2nd edn. Oxford: Oxford University Press.

Eigen, M. (1997) Being too good. In M. Rock (ed.), *Psychodynamic Supervision. Perspectives of the Supervisor and the Supervisee*. New Jersey: Jason Aronson Inc.

Fonagy, P. and Target, M. (1998) Mentalization and the changing aims of child psychoanalysis. *Psychoanalytic Dialogues*, 8(1), 87–114.

Fordham, M. (1961). Suggestions towards a theory of supervision. *Journal of Analytical Psychology*, 6.

Gibson, W. and Pope, K. (1993) The ethics of counselling: a national survey of certified counsellors. *Journal of Counselling and Development*, 71, 330–6.

Hawkins, P. and Shohet, R. (1989) *Supervision in the Helping Professions*. Buckingham: Open University Press.

Henderson, P. (2001) Supervising counsellors in primary care. In S. Wheeler and D. King (eds), *Supervising Counsellors. Issues of Responsibility*. London: Sage.

Hickey, A. (2005) Risky business? A study of the primary care counsellor and assessment for risk of harm. *Counsellors and Psychotherapists in Primary Care*, 6(2), 8–9.

Hinshelwood, R. D. and Skogstad, W. (2002) Psychic pain in health-care organisations. *Psychoanalytic Psychotherapy*, 16(2), 110–24.

Hopkins, S. and O'Callaghan, M. (1999) Doctors, counsellors and their patients: intrapsychic and interpersonal issues. In R. Bor and D. McCan (eds), *The Practice of Counselling in Primary Care*. London: Sage.

Jenkins, P. (2001) Supervisory responsibility and the law. In S. Wheeler and D. King (eds), *Supervising Counsellors. Issues of Responsibility*. London: Sage.

Jones, H., Murphy, A., Neaman, G., Tollermache, R. and Vasserman, D. (1994) Psychotherapy and counselling in a GP practice: making use of the setting. *British Journal of Psychotherapy*, 10(4), 543–51.

Jones, R. (1989) Supervision: a choice between equals? *British Journal of Psychotherapy*, 5(4), 505–11.

Keithley, J., Bond, T. and Marsh, G. (2002) Conclusions. In J. Keithley, T. Bond and G. Marsh (eds), *Counselling in Primary Care*, 2nd edn. Oxford: Oxford University Press.

Keats, J. (1817) Letter to his brothers. In J. Mee (ed.), *Selected Letters*. Oxford: Oxford University Press (2002).

King, D. (2001) Clinical responsibility and the supervision of counsellors. In S. Wheeler and D. King (eds), *Supervising Counsellors. Issues of Responsibility*. London: Sage.

King, D. and Wheeler, S. (1998) Counselling supervision: to regulate or not to regulate? *Counselling*, 9(4), 306–10.

King, D. and Wheeler, S. (1999) The responsibilities of counsellor supervisors: a qualitative study. *British Journal of Guidance and Counselling*, 27(2), 215–29.

Knight, J. (2003) Reflections on the therapist–supervisor relationship. In J. Wiener, R. Mizen and J. Duckham (eds), *Supervising and Being Supervised. A Practice in Search of a Theory*. Basingstoke: Palgrave Macmillan.

Lane, R. C. (1990) The recalcitrant supervisee: the negative supervisory reaction. In R. C. Lane (ed.), *Psychoanalytic Approaches to Supervision*. New York: Brunner/Mazel.

Lawson, B. (2000) Rethinking Supervision. *Counselling*, September, 486–7.

Lees, J. (1997) An approach to counselling in GP surgeries. *Psychodynamic Counselling*, 3(1), 33–48.

Lidmila, A. (1997) Shame, knowledge and modes of enquiry in supervision. In G. Shipton (ed.), *Supervision of Psychotherapy and Counselling*. Buckingham: Open University Press.

Litton, R. (2001) Don't court disaster. *Effective Counselling*, August, 1–5.

Mander, G. (1998) Dyads and triads: some thoughts on the nature of therapy supervision. In P. Clarkson (ed.), *Supervision. Psychoanalytic and Jungian Perspectives*. London: Whurr.

Mander, G. (2002) Supervision of supervision: specialism or new profession? In C. Driver and E. Martin (eds), *Supervising Psychotherapy*. London: Sage.

Martin, E. (2002) Giving, taking, stealing: the ethics of supervision. In C. Driver and E. Martin (eds), *Supervising Psychotherapy: Psychoanalytic and Psychodynamic Perspectives*. London: Sage.

Martin, E. (2005) The unconscious in supervision. In C. Driver and E. Martin (eds) *Supervision and the Analytic Attitude*. London: Whurr.

Mattinson, J. (1975) *The Reflection Process in Casework Supervision*, 2nd edn. London: Tavistock Institute of Marital Studies.

Mollon, P. (1997) Supervision: a space for thinking. In G. Shipton (ed.), *Supervision of Psychotherapy and Counselling*. Buckingham: Open University Press.

Parrott, C. (1999) Doing therapy briefly in primary care: clinical applications. In R. Bor and D. McCan (eds), *The Practice of Counselling in Primary Care*. London: Sage.

Perry, C. (2003) Into the labyrinth: a developing approach to supervision. In J. Wiener, R. Mizen and J. Duckham (eds), *Supervising and Being Supervised. A Practice in Search of a Theory*. Basingstoke: Palgrave Macmillan.

Pickvance, D. (1997) Becoming a supervisor. In G. Shipton (ed.), *Supervision of Psychotherapy and Counselling*. Buckingham: Open University Press.

Riesenberg-Malcom, R. (2001) Bion's theory of containment. In C. Bronstein (ed.), *Kleinian Theory: A Contemporary Perspective*. London: Whurr.

Rock, M. H. (1997) *Psychodynamic Supervision. Perspectives of the Supervisor and the Supervisee*. New Jersey: Jason Aronson Inc.

Searles, H. (1979) *Countertransference and Related Subjects*. Madison, WI: International Universities Press.

Shane, M. and Shane, E. (1995) Un-American activities and other dilemmas experienced in the supervision of candidates. *Psychoanalytic Inquiry*, 15, 226–39.

Sivyer, J. (2003) A tug of war within counselling? *CPC Review*, 4(2), 7.

South Derbyshire Health Authority (1996) *Report of the Inquiry into the Care of Anthony Smith*. Derby: Southern Derbyshire Health Authority and Derbyshire County Council.

Stewart, J. (2002) The interface between teaching and supervision. In C. Driver and E. Martin (eds), *Supervising Psychotherapy*. London: Sage.

Stewart, N. (2004) Supervising the primary care counsellor within the psychodynamic frame. *Psychodynamic Practice*, 10(3), 354–72.

Szecsody, I. (1990) Supervision: a didactic or mutative situation. *Psychoanalytic Psychotherapy*, 4(3), 245–61.

Thomas, M. (2005) Through the looking glass: creativity in supervision. In C. Driver and E. Martin (eds), *Supervision and the Analytic Attitude*. London: Whurr.

Thomas, S. (2005) Supervision and training: two different foci. In C. Driver and E. Martin (eds), *Supervision and the Analytic Attitude*. London: Whurr.

Wake, L. (2005) Keynote speech to the United Kingdom Council for Psychotherapy Annual General Meeting.

Wheeler, S. (2000). *British Association for Counselling and Psychotherapy Journal*, 11(6), 334–5.

Wheeler, S. and King, D. (eds) (2001) *Supervising Counsellors. Issues of Responsibility*. London: Sage.

Wiener, J. and Sher, M. (1988) Assessment for counselling and treatment options. In J. Wiener and M. Sher (eds), *Counselling and Psychotherapy in Primary Health Care: A Psychodynamic Approach*. London: Macmillan Press.

Winnicott, D. W. (1949) Hate in the countertransference. In D. W. Winnicott, *Through Paediatrics to Psychoanalysis*. London: Hogarth Press (1975).

Winnicott, D. W. (1960) Countertransference. In D. W. Winnicott, *The Maturational Processes and the Facilitating Environment*. London: Hogarth Press (1965).

Winnicott, D. W. (1963) Casework and mental illness. In D. W. Winnicott, *The Maturational Processes and the Facilitating Environment*. London: Hogarth Press (1965).

Wolff, H. (1971) The therapeutic and developmental functions of psychotherapy. *British Journal Medical Psychology*, 44, 117–30.

Zarbarfi, A. (2000) Counselling across social, sexual and ethnic differences. In J. Keithley, T. Bond and G. Marsh (eds), *Counselling in Primary Care*, 2nd edn. Oxford: Oxford University Press.

Zinkin, L. (1995) Supervision: the impossible profession. In P. Kugler (ed.), *Jungian Perspectives on Clinical Supervision*. Switzerland: Daimon.

CHAPTER TEN

Placements and Mentoring for Primary Care Counselling in Today's NHS

Christine Driscoll

THIS chapter discusses two aspects of counselling practice[1] in primary care: placements and mentoring for trainee and newly qualified counsellors, with a focus on systems that promote working practices to develop and support counsellors and therefore safe counselling practice.

All professions in health care recognise the need for students to be exposed to a positive learning experience in the workplace that marries theory into practice, supports practitioners and builds confidence at the same time as addressing areas of competence without compromising patient safety. Systems that cross organisational boundaries are in place to assure the quality of the learning experience for the student, at the same time addressing issues such as assessment and competence. The newly qualified also need support and development in the workplace and access to systems such as induction, supervision, ongoing training and mentoring.

Currently in industry and the professions alike, there is a

growing emergence of the value of mentoring in the workplace. Mentor schemes are run in a variety of settings, such as industry, education, schools, youth work and health care. The terms mentor and mentoring can be confusing and organisations or professions have different definitions or purposes for mentoring. Most of the definitions contain words such as 'support, help, learning, making transitions and realising potential'. Successful mentoring schemes are introduced into organisations or services in a structured and planned way, alongside training and development interventions for managers, mentors and mentees.

Clutterbuck and Klasen (2002) describe mentoring as a 'means of assisting transitions in thinking patterns' and 'a developmental conversation' that has the potential to create opportunities for learning and development for both the mentor and mentee. The Standing Committee on Postgraduate Medical and Dental Education (SCOPME, 1998) offers a definition of mentoring as

> a process whereby an experienced, highly regarded, empathic person, the mentor, guides another, the mentee, in the development or examination of their own ideas, learning and personal development. The mentor, who often, but not necessarily, works in the same organisation or field as the mentee, achieves this by listening and talking in confidence to the mentee.

Both of these definitions seem to embrace the notion of a formative process or developmental mentoring and agree that mentoring can be a useful intervention for helping with transitions in the workplace.

The Counselling and Psychotherapy Forum for Primary Care has produced a person specification for trainees, alongside minimum training standards for primary care counsellors for organisations to use. The function of mentoring offered is:

> Clinical placements are best offered under the guidance of a mentor. The mentor must be an experienced practice counsellor

> working in the same or another practice. The provision of mentoring is distinct from clinical supervision and involves various components such as assessment of suitable patients, teaching training and management of the placement.

This brings to mentoring practice the management of the placement and assessment of patients.

A definition that is most akin to this is used for student nurses guided by the professional body that regulates nursing. The Nursing and Midwifery Council (NMC) states: 'A mentor is a nurse, midwife or specialist community public health nurse who facilitates learning and supervises and assesses students in a practice setting' (NMC, 2005). This definition shifts the emphasis in mentoring to include supervision and assessment of practice. This shift towards summative assessment can impact on power dynamics and has the potential to diminish the developmental element of the mentoring relationship.

From these definitions we can see the emergence of three models of mentoring:

- developmental formative mentoring for new roles, transitions and career development;
- counselling mentoring, which includes assessment of suitable patients and management of the placement;
- in nurse education mentoring, which includes teaching and elements of summative assessment.

All models emphasise the intentionally supportive learning nature of the one-to-one relationship. Further discussion of mentoring takes place later in the chapter.

Primary Care: The Context

It is worth noting some of the complex issues that make up general practice and that have led to primary care counselling emerging as a speciality in the field.

Trainee and newly qualified counsellors who work in primary care will work in a setting commonly known as the GP practice or the practice. General practice consists of a number of individual independent organisations of different sizes, e.g. single-handed doctors or larger groups of doctors working in partnership. The doctors via the practice employ the practice staff, i.e. nurses and receptionists. In the main, most other health care professionals, such as health visitors, midwives or district nurses, are attached to practices but are employed by a health care provider organisation such as a primary care trust. Current government policies are designed to align general practice with working practices in the NHS through a set of common organisational, employment and clinical governance quality standards, while at the same time keeping the independent contractual status of general practice. Other policies impacting on general practice are, for example, meeting access targets for patients, the extended role of nurses, nurse prescribing, patient choice and current drivers for commissioning services for patients.

General practice sits within primary care, with its emphasis on health, but the essence of general practice is based on a medical model of care that includes diagnosis, treatment and cure. Everyone registered with a practice, both ill and well, is viewed as a patient. Many general practitioners may have limited experience in dealing with healing of the emotional aspect of an individual's health. The caseload for counsellors is therefore potentially everyone who is registered with the practice.

Primary care counselling has also been organised in different ways. Historically some practices identified the need for a counselling service and were prepared to commission counsellors to do this work; other practices chose not to purchase counselling or did not identify the need for local counselling provision. This has led to a disparate range of counselling service provision not based on a systematic identified health needs assessment for a given population. Currently the need for counselling is greater than the resources allocated for counselling services.

Counselling is a profession that is working towards a more formal and uniform approach to training and professional regulation. Commonly all aspects of counselling practice are underpinned by a code of ethics and code of conduct. Each individual counsellor will have been trained in different orientations and for different lengths of time. Counsellors have organised themselves in many different ways; for example, self-employed practitioners may manage a mixed caseload that crosses private, public and voluntary sectors. Therefore, issues affecting the human resource element of counselling practice, such as employment practice, placements in voluntary organisations, training placements, pay, supervision and ongoing professional development, have been handled differently for counsellors in each setting. It was very difficult for a GP practice to know exactly what it would get from having a counsellor in the practice, if the counsellor was fit to practise or what the anticipated clinical outcomes were for clients from the differing approaches to counselling.

Since 2003, counsellors who work in primary care have been more likely to work in a managed counselling service and be employed by the primary care trust. Salaries for counsellors have been banded using the newly implemented Knowledge and Skills framework and Agenda for Change pay and reward scheme in the NHS.

Today primary care is a complex, fast changing environment that brings together the different paradigms of management and education alongside professional codes of conduct and ongoing support, training and development in the NHS. This poses opportunities and challenges for all staff who work in primary care.

What Helps to Support Trainees and Newly Qualified Practitioners?

The learning that happens in the workplace is of paramount importance for trainees and newly qualified staff. It is here that they are exposed to the culture of a profession, team or organisation while learning. All health care professions offer different practice placements as an essential component of the student's experience and development of practice towards competence, qualification, building professional identity and role authority. Health care organisations and the professions also recognise that newly qualified practitioners need access to systems that enable them to build their confidence and competence at work, enter the post-qualification phase and embrace the journey of continuous professional development and life-long learning.

In nursing it is an expectation that the work of teaching and growing the next generation. The assessment of competence in the practice setting sits with existing practitioners, who share their skills and knowledge with students. NMC states: 'Nurses and midwives on the NMC professional register have a duty to facilitate students of nursing and midwifery and others to develop their competence' (NMC, 2005, section 6.4). A policy paper from the Department of Health (2001a) sets out standards for placements for both pre (undergraduate) and post registration (postgraduate) students. The guidance includes standards for providing practice placements, the practice as a learning environment, student support and assessment of practice. Both undergraduate and postgraduate nursing students have placements arranged and managed in service provider organisations. Each student is allocated to an assessor or mentor who carries out both formative and summative assessments in the placement. Most provider organisations have practice placement coordinators who liaise with workplace mentors or assessors and the universities.

In medicine some GP practices are designated training practices for medical students and general practitioners. To achieve that status the practice has to meet a set of rigorous standards set down by medical schools and postgraduate deaneries. The practice is then subject to regular organisational audit and assessment of the learning environment.

Some practices have embraced wholeheartedly the concept of the practice as a learning environment. This is leading to the emergence of a new approach that is aimed at all students who have placements into the practice. All students are expected to have a learning plan, which helps them to achieve and meet their learning and development needs in the placement. To facilitate this multiprofessional learning approach some GP practices have developed a resource pack for students, which outlines expectations for the practice, the practice structure, the roles and responsibilities of all staff and learning opportunities within the placement.

In nursing, therapies and medicine all placements are aimed at meeting the learning outcomes needed at a particular stage in an individuals overall training programme towards qualification. So what about counselling? As a primary care practice, it is in its infancy in working in a managed service. Traditionally placements for trainees in primary care counselling were organised by the trainees/students, with assessment of practice and competence sitting in training or educational supervision in training organisations. Organisational involvement was variable and patchy, leaving management of the local service, ongoing support and development with the counsellor. This system had the potential to leave the trainee counsellor working alone and unsupported in practice placements. This left trainees, training organisations and provider organisations with increased risks, which may have impacted negatively on client care. Counselling is part of a managed service within the NHS as a provider organisation, and this provides opportunities for counselling services to work in line with the same organisational and employment practices that support health care professionals.

For counsellors to work safely and effectively in a complex

setting such as primary care they will also need to have knowledge of:

- The primary care health team: how a practice works as a team and implications for counsellors and counselling practice.
- The organisation of local primary and secondary care, mental health and voluntary services.
- Legislative knowledge, e.g. Children's Act, health and safety at work.
- Assessment and risk assessment.
- Working with clients within a limited or fixed time frame.
- Referral pathways in and out of counselling.
- Psychotropic medicines.
- Clinical governance frameworks.
- Data protection, confidentiality and record keeping in primary care.

The knowledge required to work effectively in primary care cannot always be gained from books, because some of it is held by experienced professionals. In a placement a trainee or newly qualified practitioner needs to be supported and guided through an individual personal learning and development plan that includes access to induction, both organisational and practice, peer discussion groups to share best practice, spending time with experienced professionals from different organisations, supervision, caseload management and mentoring.

The Role of Trainees and Newly Qualified Practitioners

It is important to appreciate that students/trainees have a central role in maximising the learning opportunities available to them in placements. Although students are supernumerary in nursing and medicine, in the workplace they are expected to be active learners while in training. All students need to familiarise themselves with course and student handbooks from education providers, the purpose of the placement and anticipated learning outcomes, provider or placement expectations, guidance on contacting the placement before starting, professional guidance regarding confidentiality and code of conduct (e.g. attitude or uniform code), and must inform any patients they are working with that they are students. Any work with patients that is delegated to students needs to be appropriate to their level of skill and stage of training. Accountability for this work rests with the trained clinician.

Newly qualified staff also need support and guidance throughout a period of settling into a new role. This support is recommended in policies; in practice it is variable and can be left to individuals to arrange their own support. Inducting and valuing new staff is one of the factors that can positively affect retention.

What Does This Mean for Counselling Services and Associated Learning and Support Mechanisms?

Tables 10.1 and 10.2 outline some of the components and systems that exist in health care organisations and are worthy of attention for an effective primary care counselling service.

Systems to Support Staff across the Helping Professions

There seems to be agreement from industry and the professions that trainees and newly qualified practitioners in any field of work alike need access to a learning environment at work that supports and values the learner and newly qualified practitioners. As part of good employment practices all staff that work or are placed in organisations need access to systems that support them such as:

- line management, including appraisal and personal development planning;
- induction;
- access to training and development opportunities;
- supervision;
- mentoring;
- professional guidance or advice.

For counsellors working in a managed service in primary care some of the organisation processes, such as induction, appraisal

TABLE 10.1
Service-focused: strategy and management

Strategic service planning: health needs assessment, commissioning and workforce development

- Mental health needs assessment.
- Identifying service provision and number of counsellors needed.
- Commissioning counselling services from providers organisations; n.b. find ways of addressing vulnerable or deprived client groups who may not be registered with GP, e.g. homeless.
- Workforce planning: commissioning of appropriate number of places for counselling students from training organisations.

Managed counselling service

- Appoint manager to lead and manage counselling service – preferably one with counselling experience.
- Develop and implement counselling and supervision policy according to professional and clinical governance standards.
- Recruit and retain counsellors.
- Induction for new staff, both general and GP practice specific.
- Line management of supervisors and counsellors.
- Appraisal and personal development planning.
- Raising awareness and influencing, for example, the board, commissioning bodies, GPs, other organisations.
- Draws up and monitor contracts, e.g. between training organisations, GP practice, supervisors and trainees.
- Liaises with training organisations, identifies and manages trainees and suitable trainee placements.
- Meets health and safety requirements.
- Use of data, e.g. clinical outcomes or from audit.

Table 10.2
Systems that support the trainee: the learner in the workplace

Universities or training organisations	*Placements in practice*	*Supervision*	*Mentoring*
Provide courses/ education experience for students who want to work in primary care	Provide evidence of health/clinical need for local practice-based counselling service	Defines model and practice for supervision	Defines model and practice for mentoring
		Training and supervision for supervisees and supervisors	Recruits and trains appropriate mentors
Educate counsellors in training	Raise awareness with provider organisations, e.g. PCT, interested in having counsellor placement	Trained supervisor with knowledge and experience of primary care counselling and brief therapy	Ability to understand the difference between supervision, line management and mentoring
Audit the quality of the learning environment or placements			
	Meet set standards, e.g. training practice or working towards them	n.b.: One hour of supervision to every six hours of clinical practice with flexibility	
Draw up a contract with partnership provider organisations for placements and monitor contract			Knowledge of how primary care works
			The time and interest to undertake a mentoring role
	Provide room for counselling to take place		
Address issues with students who may be failing			
	Manage environmental safety, e.g. lone working		Mentee awareness of scheme and benefits
Identify and support students with special needs			
			Mentor and mentee matching
	Work with or implement PCT guidelines and policies that meet professional counselling standards, PCT and practice		
Train and develop mentors			
			The contract is drawn up and works within a time-limited contractual

governance issues, such as record keeping, data protection and collection, feedback to referrer	learning framework
	Evaluates relationship with mentee
	Support such as group supervision for mentors
Raise awareness of service and its parameters in whole practice team and clients	
Make appropriate referrals to counselling service	
For trainees	
Welcome and induction to practice and learning opportunities, encourage self assessment	
Early identification of poor performance or problems – to discuss with trainee and line manager	

and mentoring, will be relatively new. This provides an opportunity for counselling managers positively to influence and shape the service and associated support mechanisms to support staff, students and newly qualified practitioners.

A policy document from the DoH (2001b) set plans for all staff who work in the NHS to participate in annual appraisal, which helps to facilitate the production of a meaningful personal development plan. Appraisal for doctors is a relatively new concept and for general practitioners is a formative process carried out by a peer who helps a colleague, the appraisee, to review his or her work as a doctor and develop a personal development plan.

What this means in practice is that each employed member of staff in the NHS in partnership with the line manager needs to develop and agree a set of work-based goals or objectives alongside a personal development/learning plan. These two components give individuals a direction for their work and learning plan for the year. For newly qualified staff or for staff starting new roles a mentoring arrangement can be an invaluable source of support. For medicine, nursing and allied health professionals most training and development opportunities happen in the workplace, on specific identified training opportunities or through systems such as learning from peers, reading, e-based learning, supervision, coaching and mentoring.

Mentoring

Historically the term mentor was associated with someone who was seen as a 'wise and trusted advisor'. In industry and the professions mentoring consisted of a relationship between a senior older person who supported and developed a younger junior person as a protégé. This relationship was based on patronage and implicitly the protégé expected personal and professional opportunities to become available because of connections with the mentor. The notion of patronage in the public sector is less acceptable because of its power to exclude sections of the workforce. Mentoring has moved away from being an informal process to a more structured and managed process.

It is helpful for services and organisations to define the difference between mentoring, coaching and counselling and to articulate what is not mentoring. There is broad agreement in the literature on the separate functions of counselling, mentoring, supervision and coaching. Counselling focuses more on helping people to understand themselves or to come to terms with issues in their personal or working lives that may manifest as personal dilemmas or problems. Mentoring works best when the focus is looking towards the future with an encouragement to commit to learning goals and extend thinking. Supervision provides a reflective space for examining aspects of work and clinical practice with clients. Coaching helps more with developing or adding to an individual's existing set of skills to do a particular job.

At the beginning of this chapter we outlined three models of mentoring, which are now further detailed.

- developmental formative mentoring for new roles, transitions and career development;
- counselling mentoring, including assessment of suitable patients and management of the placement;
- nurse education mentoring, including teaching and elements of summative assessment.

Developmental mentoring is a process that facilitates learning and development through a relationship that is entered into voluntarily by both parties, i.e. the mentor and the mentee, and is underpinned by trust, confidentiality and mutual respect. The main focus of the mentoring relationship is about you at work, such as career development or taking on and establishing a new role. The mentor's role is to help the mentee to develop at work, extend thinking and broaden horizons. Mentors may also share organisational and professional knowledge and experience. In the mentoring relationship a learning contract is established that recognises the mentees taking responsibility for their learning. The contract includes elements such as the length of the contract, how often, for how long and where meetings happen, other support offered during the relationship, such as e-mail or telephone support, the focus of the work in the sessions, what records are kept and how the work will be reviewed. The boundaries between line management, mentoring and mentee performance can be explored and clarified.

The concept and practice of developmental mentoring is in its infancy in both medicine and nursing. However, it is more acceptable for senior nurses, therapists and health care managers. Doctors sometimes find it difficult to acknowledge that they may need help for themselves at work or at times in their career. The culture in medicine has been of self-reliance, doctor knows best, clinical independence. The model of education used in medicine focuses more on building technical skills and knowledge and the application of evidence-based medicine. This is very different from the spirit of the learner-centred approach through a mentoring relationship. An evaluation of a mentoring scheme run by the London University medical deanery found that doctors are slowly beginning to accept the value of mentoring as a concept and practice.

Nurse education mentoring adds another dimension to mentoring that explicitly includes teaching and elements of summative assessment. The mentor is required to offer the student support and guidance in the practice area, helping the mentee to make sense of his or her practice through application of theory, assessing, evaluating and giving feedback and facilitating reflection on practice, performance and experience. The mentor is viewed as a positive role model and assesses fitness to practice and the breadth and depth of knowledge required to be awarded a diploma or degree. Mentors add to the quality assurance element of the placement by creating a positive learning environment and contributing to educational audit of placements. Mentors are expected to be experienced practitioners who have attended specific training to become a mentor and attend mentor updates. The practice of group supervision or learning sets is a relatively new and emerging support mechanism for the mentor role.

Placements providers are expected to provide time for mentors to meet their students; this can be challenging for organisations and mentors alike in attempting to balance existing workloads with meeting the needs of students. This system is well established in nursing but it is not without its challenges. Current debates in nursing involve issues such as protecting time for mentors, improving the quality of the work-based placement as a learning environment and addressing the issues of students who are failing.

The training standards set out by the Counselling and Psychotherapy Forum for Primary Care offers another dimension to mentoring practice for trainees that includes assessment of suitable patients and management of the placement. This adds an element of management to the mentor role. The standard suggests that the mentor needs to be an experienced counsellor who can undertake the work of a mentor. Challenges will come from implementation of the standards in a small service. For example, how will counselling resource activities such as mentoring and supervision from within an existing pool of mainly part-time staff? What are the differences or potential overlaps or tensions between mentoring, line management, educational supervision and counsellor competence in meeting the proposed standard? What training will experienced counsellors need to help them to become successful mentors?

Implementing Mentoring in Health Care Professions and Organisations

Commonality exists across the literature about organising mentoring schemes, the benefits of mentoring and the skills and qualities of mentors and mentees. The benefits of mentoring schemes can extend to both mentors and mentees. For example, for mentees, increased personal confidence may help to speed career progress, open the mentee to new ways of thinking, and mentors might gain increased interpersonal skills from training. The organisational benefits of mentoring schemes may be a mixture of the following components: improved recruitment and retention of staff, quicker induction of new staff, improved networking and communication and reinforcement of cultural change.

To implement mentoring successfully a number of issues need to be addressed. Organisations, services or professions need to identify the need and purpose of a mentoring scheme. This would include stakeholder discussions about the benefits of mentoring, who can access the scheme and who can become a mentor. Resources would need to be set aside to lead and manage the mentoring scheme, for training for mentors and mentees and for time to publicise and raise awareness of all staff of the scheme and its benefits. Staff will want to know if mentoring is to be carried out within existing roles and time or if there is protected time and financial remuneration.

Who can be a mentor depends on the type of mentoring scheme chosen. Potential mentors are people who trust and respect others and who are trusted and respected, interested in developing others and committed to their own learning and development, and who can commit the time to the role of mentor. Clutterbuck suggests that mentors need two basic skills: first, the ability to be quiet and listen and the capacity to give only of their experience when it is clear how this will guide the mentee; second, the ability to be flexible and to adjust how they respond according to the mentee's need and circumstances. In other words, this means being and staying mentee focused – a challenge indeed for health care professionals who may spend much of their working lives responding to and giving information and advice.

For mentoring to be successful it is essential that the mentors are trained and supported in that role and that mentees are trained and understand how to make the most of a mentoring relationship. The following elements inform the basis of an initial mentor-training programme:

- Making the mentoring relationship work: the capacity to build and maintain effective one-to-one relationships.
- Developing a learning contract: exploring and setting learning goals.
- Exploring boundaries with other systems such as line managers and supervisors.
- Work with the mentee: face-to-face sessions, e-mail, telephone contact.
- Confidentiality: guarding of personal information, keeping professional and organisational codes of conduct for confidentiality.
- Active listening skills: listening to the words, feelings and meanings through use of reflection, clarifying and paraphrasing.
- Self-awareness and the capacity to stay mentee focused, e.g. focusing on the needs of the mentee by not giving too much advice or telling personal stories.
- Support and challenge skills.
- Ability to give feedback.
- Ability to ask useful questions that help reflection and enable the mentee to move on.
- Record keeping: agreeing what or if any records are kept.
- What happens when things don't go as planned: managing the breakdown of a mentoring relationship.
- Ending and evaluation.

Being a mentor does not suit everyone and a training or development programme may need to have the capacity to identify trainee mentors who are less suited to a mentoring role. More training and development needs may merge as mentoring is embedded. It is worth considering what ongoing support and development mentors need: for example, group supervision, participating in a learning set or developing a critical friend or peer review mode with a mentor colleague.

For many executives, managers and health care professionals who want to become mentors the biggest challenge is to work in a different paradigm from their current role or profession. For counsellors it may be that the challenge will be to view the mentees as colleagues and not clients.

What Next?

This chapter has raised awareness of issues affecting trainees and newly qualified staff in health care settings and provides some triggers for newly managed counselling services in primary care. It has not addressed all the issues and further questions or topics will need discussion as services change and develop. Counselling services may want to use best practice about workforce planning and development in implementing a service that is fit for practice and addresses recruitment and retention.

It may be useful to ask some of the following questions.

- What needs to happen to prepare the existing workforce to meet the needs of new staff and trainees in counselling?
- How similar or different is mentoring in counselling to existing systems such as supervision and line management?
- How are and by whom are systems such as performance and appraisal carried out in a managed counselling service? For example, who, using what evidence, would sign a counsellor through a gateway on the Agenda for Change pay structure?
- What contractual arrangements are needed for placements between training organisations, NHS organisations and trainees about expectations and the management of issues such as sickness, health and safety and, ultimately, performance?

Some of these questions and issues will be addressed as counselling in the NHS implements the standards set out by the Counselling and Psychotherapy Forum for Primary Care Person Specification Criteria and its Minimum Training Standards for Primary Care Counsellors and the profession moves towards regulation and revalidation.

Summary

This chapter has attempted to highlight issues relating to effective placements and support for trainee and newly qualified counsellors. The complexities of managing the placement for trainees and newly qualified staff are challenging and are a vital part of managing and developing a workforce that is fit for practice and retains staff. The discussions have focused on the challenges for primary care, placements for trainee counsellors and challenges and opportunities for trainees, practice placements and training organisations alike. In conclusion, students or trainees in a profession need a rich effective work-based placement that offers elements of formative and summative assessment and access to the knowledge held by experienced practitioners.

More organisational and structural changes are on the horizon for education providers and the NHS and consequently for primary care trusts and mental health services. This means that all organisations will need to work in partnership to provide effective service provision that addresses the quality of the trainee counsellor's experiences, and short- and long-term career plans that will help with recruitment and retention. Implementing such systems could then offer some degree of containment to counsellors and ultimately clients, no matter what organisation structure is in place.

Note

1 The term 'primary care counselling' – sometimes shortened to counselling – is used as a shorthand for all the psychological therapies used in primary care, including counselling, psychotherapy and psychology, and applies to counselling carried out within a general practice setting.

References

Bower, P., Foster, J. and Mellor-Clark, J. (2001) *Quality in Counselling in Primary Care: A Guide for Effective Commissioning and Clinical Governance*. National Research and Development Centre.

Chambers, R. et al. (2005) *Good Mentoring Toolkit*. London: Radcliffe Press.

Clutterbuck, D. and Klasen, N. (2002) *Implementing Mentoring Schemes*. Oxford: Butterworth Heinemann.

Counselling and Psychotherapy Forum for Primary Care (2001a) *Minimum Training Standards for Primary Care Counselling*. Brighton: Counselling and Psychotherapy Forum for Primary Care.

Counselling and Psychotherapy Forum for Primary Care (2001b) *Person Specification Criteria*. Brighton: Counselling and Psychotherapy Forum for Primary Care.

Department of Health (2001a) *Placements in Focus*. London: HMSO.

Department of Health (2001b) *Working Together – Learning Together*. London: HMSO.

Department of Health (2003) *Delivering Investment in General Practice – Implementing the New GMS Contract*. London: HMSO.

Department of Health (2004) *Mentoring for Doctors: Enhancing the Benefit*. London: HMSO.

Doherty, C. and Hanmer, O. (2004) *Mentoring for Doctors in Primary and Secondary Care*.

Egan, G. (1994) *The Skilled Helper*. London: Brooks/Cole.

Heron, J. (1989) *The Facilitator's Handbook*. London: Kogan Page.

Heron, J. (1990) *Helping the Client*. London: Sage.

Megginson, D. and Clutterbuck, D. (1995) *Mentoring in Action*. London: Kogan Page.

Megginson, D. and Clutterbuck, D. (2005) *Techniques for Coaching and Mentoring*. London: Elsevier.

NMC (2005) *Code of Professional Conduct*. London: Nursing and Midwifery Council.

Parsloe, E. and Wray, M. (2000) *Coaching and Mentoring*. London: Kogan Page.

Royal College of Nursing (2005) *Guidance for Mentors of Student Nurses and Midwives*. London: RCN.

SCOPME (1998) *Supporting Doctors and Dentists at Work: An Inquiry into Mentoring*. London: Standing Committee on Postgraduate Medical and Dental Education.

Secretary of State for Employment and Secretary of State for Education and Science (1986) *Working Together – Education and Training*. White Paper. London: HMSO.

UK Resource Centre for Women in Science, Engineering and Technology (2004) *Good Mentoring Guide*. London: UKRC.

Useful Resources for Mentoring

BMA, exploring mentoring: www.bma.org.uk

BMJ, get yourself connected: www.studentbmj.com

Royal College of General Practitioners: www.rcgp.org.uk

Royal College of Nursing: www.rcn.org.uk

Department of Health, information on DoH policy about learning and CPD: www.dh.gov.uk/policyandguidance/HumanResourcesandTraining/learning

CIPD, the HR development website: www.cipd.co.uk

Clutterbuck Associates: www.clutterbuckassociates.com

European Mentoring and Coaching Council: www.emcouncil.org.uk

The Coaching and Mentoring Network: www.coachingnetwork.org.uk

Doherty Associates, mentor development: cdoherty@dohertyassociates.fsnet.co.uk

CHAPTER ELEVEN

Continuing Professional Development

Fit for Practice

Maureen Moore

THE aim of this chapter is to explore the issues relating to the maintenance of the quality of counselling provision through the endeavours of the individual counsellor. It is hoped that this will contribute to counsellors' understanding of the impact that they have on their own clinical practice, the outcome of their clinical work and the overall reputation of counselling as a respected profession.

In recent years continuing professional development (CPD) has become increasingly more important and relevant to all professionals. The demand for higher standards in the delivery of counselling and psychological therapies has become progressively greater, as indicated by the number of extended training courses and degree level qualifications. This emphasis on CPD became increasingly prominent in the 1990s as professional associations required members to adhere to a policy of maintaining currency through CPD. What was once voluntary and recognised as 'good practice' has become a requirement for continuing professional practice. For example, during 2000 the British Psychological Society (BPS) voted to make CPD mandatory.

UNESCO vigorously promoted the notion of life-long learning as a strategy for managing the pace of change in the 1970s. Initially, the term 'continuing education' was used, but Richard Gardner (1978, pp. 2–3) proposed the term 'continuing professional development', which had a wider application, including pure education as well as development of the individual's persona and the advancement of his or her professional career. Gardner's suggestion that learning activities should include learning from experience and practice meant that organisations too needed to develop a positive learning ethos.

Counselling and psychotherapy have increased in acceptance as treatment methods for a wide range of common life problems as well as a recommended form of treatment for more complex mental health problems in primary care. Indeed, recent recommendations from the National Institute for Clinical Excellence have highlighted the relevance of the psychological therapies for anxiety, depression and more recently post-traumatic stress disorder (PTSD).

Primary care trusts now recognise the predominance of patients presenting with issues that have psychological implications as well as physical aspects. General practitioners have limited time in which to respond to the concerns expressed by patients and for the most part they have minimal psychological training to support their interventions.

The NHS Agenda for Change is a new pay system designed to ensure fair pay and a system for career progression. Staff will be paid on the basis of the jobs they do, which will be linked to the skills and knowledge they apply to those roles. Career progression and personal development are integral parts of the system and supported by the Knowledge and Skills Framework, linked to periodic professional reviews, enabling individuals and their employers to identify appropriate CPD. Counselling is now included in this pay system in recognition of the increasing role of counsellors as a necessary component of health care provided at both the primary and tertiary levels of the health service.

Counsellors working in primary care are encountering clients who have complex presentations emerging from the relationship between their physical, social and emotional needs. In addition, counsellors in the health service practice in a multiprofessional setting and must be aware of the moral, ethical and legal requirements of that context in relation to patient care.

The question of 'quality of service' is central to effective care provision. In 1989, Welsh and Woodward highlighted the issues of incompetence and negligence and the expectations of the public with regard to effective service in their report on the National Strategy for Continuing Professional Development. Shortly after that publication the National Health Service and Community Care Act 1990 was passed. It required health practitioners to provide a widening range of services for the community. The year 1999 saw the introduction of the Health Act, which introduced the concept of clinical governance. This was described in the preceding White Paper (1997) as 'actions to ensure that risks are avoided, adverse events are rapidly disseminated and systems are in place to ensure continuous improvements in clinical care'. Clinical governance was reinforced by the 'statutory duty of quality' provision by NHS trusts and primary care providers. This duty required health providers and practitioners to monitor and audit their work. An essential part of the implementation of clinical governance was 'life-long learning' through locally managed CPD programmes. The NHS White Paper of 1997 also strengthened the requirement for professional self-regulation.

It is of no surprise that there is now a demand by professional associations, employers and patients for continuing formal maintenance and monitoring of the competence of counsellors and psychotherapists.

What Is Continuing Professional Development?

There are many definitions of CPD, each highlighting different aspects of essential learning and developmental activities depending on the profession from which it is emerging. An early definition adopted by the Construction Industry Council in 1986 read: 'CPD is the systematic maintenance, improvement and broadening of knowledge and skill and the development of personal qualities necessary for the execution of professional and technical duties throughout the practitioner's working life.' However, for the purpose of consistency across the health-related professions the definition provided by the Health Professions Council (HPC) is adopted here to describe the purpose and function of CPD. The HPC defines CPD as: 'a range of learning activities through which professionals maintain and develop throughout their career to ensure that they retain their capacity to practise safely, effectively and legally within their evolving scope of practice' (HPC consultation document, p. 7). An alternative helpful definition is provided by the Professional Associations Research Network (PARN). CPD is defined by that research-based organisation as 'any process or activity that provides added value to the capability of the professional through the increase in knowledge, skills and personal qualities necessary for the appropriate execution of professional and technical duties, often termed competence'. In all definitions there is reference to activities that increase knowledge, skills and personal qualities with the intention of improving practice.

What Is the Purpose of CPD?

> Everything flows and everything is constantly changing. You cannot step twice in the same river, for other waters are constantly flowing on.
>
> Heraclitus

Freidman et al. (2000) identify four intended outcomes of CPD. These relate to the need to ensure secure professional practice within a changing world, to assure the public of the currency and validity of professional practice and to offer employers a measure of competence in its workforce.

Professional associations employ CPD policies that require their registered or accredited members to 'participate in continuous, focused learning activities'. This emphasis is designed to ensure career development for its members, to facilitate adaptation to changes and finally to improve the quality of professional practice. The practice of promoting and facilitating professional learning relies on the introduction of new knowledge and skills and the understanding that comes from sharing of experiences and insights between professionals. This process is in the best interest of the public, who will be assured of the continued competence of association members, is an indication of the integrity of the professional associations that monitor the quality of its members and ultimately is also for the benefit of the members, who will, in the process, improve and maintain their skills, knowledge and qualities beyond initial entry requirements (Eraut, 1994). CPD is a fundamental requirement for professional accreditation and/or registration and failure to maintain the level of CPD required by the professional association to which you belong may constitute a breach of professional ethics.

The United Kingdom Council for Psychotherapists (UKCP) aligns itself with other organisations and professions that place strong emphasis upon verifiable CPD by including the following statement in Section 2.8 of its Ethical Guidelines: 'Psychotherapists are required to maintain their ability to perform competently and to take the necessary steps to do so.' Member organisations of UKCP manage their CPD requirements differently. For example, some use the testimony of professional networks or groups meeting to discuss and agree the CPD programme for each individual, whereas others require a proportion of CPD learning activities to be accredited CPD hours.

The British Association for Counselling and Psychotherapy (BACP), in its Ethical Framework for Good Practice (2002) also recommends that: 'a commitment to good practice requires practitioners to keep up to date with the latest knowledge and respond to changing circumstances. They should consider carefully their own need for continuing professional development and engage in appropriate educational activities.' The accreditation criteria for BACP require registrants to provide evidence of continued reflective practice and require the individual counsellor's supervisor to give testimony to the planning and implementation of the CPD process.

Counselling and Psychotherapists in Primary Care (CPC) requires that 'All Registered and Intermediate Members commit to their ongoing Professional Development of 30 hours a year.' This is monitored by an annual CPD statement signed by the member.

The British Psychology Society (BPS) requires practising chartered psychologists to begin CPD when they start to offer services to the public. This requirement is an extension of the basic principle in the Society's Code of Conduct (Clause 2): 'Psychologists shall endeavour to maintain and develop their professional competence, to recognise and work within its limits, and to identify and ameliorate factors which restrict it.'

All professions, in particular those associated with the promotion, prevention and maintenance of health or with the care and rehabilitation of others, require their practitioners to participate in CPD. Key to the acceptance of any health-related profession for regulation by a regulator is the standard of training and conduct of its practitioners. Even more crucial is the central role that CPD will play in the success of professional regulation as a method of protecting the public. Existing models indicate that any regulatory authority will require practitioners wishing to maintain their registration with a regulating authority to provide evidence of CPD.

The Health Professions Council (HPC), a regulator currently

responsible for maintaining standards of professionals registered with it, requires new professions to show that they meet the Council's ten criteria for assessing the readiness of new professions for statutory regulation. One of those criteria reads: 'The Aspirant group/s must – *Be committed to continuous professional development.*' The HPC considers that in order to protect the public it must require individual registrants to commit themselves to enhancement of their own professional development and that employers must also recognise the value of CPD. For example, in order to remain registered with the HPC, approved procedure indicates that registrants are required to adhere to those standards set for the profession. The standards form the basis on which registrants' 'fitness to practise' will be determined.

The HPC, together with professional associations, providers of training and employers, agreed key obligations of registrants with regard to CPD. Current requirements for registration include:

- maintenance of a continuous, up-to-date and accurate record of CPD activities;
- evidence that CPD activities are a mixture of learning activities relevant to current or future practice;
- CPD planning that shows that CPD has contributed to the quality of practice and service delivery;
- CPD planning that shows that CPD benefits the service user;
- ability to present a written portfolio containing evidence of CPD upon request.

These requirements are indicators of the centrality of CPD to professional practice regardless of the nature of the work undertaken or the regulating authority. Similar CPD criteria will apply to those who are in practice, education, management and/or research in respect of the profession in which they are registered. The responsibility, therefore, to maintain a level of knowledge and skill and an attitude appropriate to the practice of counselling is on not only those who are in direct contact with clients on a daily basis but all who would be registered as professional practitioners and all those who would be involved in the continued professionalism of counselling and psychotherapy. This is an important consideration because of the range of roles that psychological therapists play in the provision of their therapeutic work. The choice of CPD is, of necessity, a combination of a search for personal development and a need to meet the challenges of the context in which the work is done.

Freidman's (Freidman et al., 2000) investigations into the definitions of CPD provided by a range of professional associations showed that CPD should be systematic and should address skills, knowledge and personal qualities. He noted the emphasis on career development rather than merely keeping abreast of new developments. Vaughan (1991, p. 5) suggested that professional associations were in the best position to verify CPD, but did not minimise the responsibility of individuals for planning their own CPD programmes. This theme was taken up by Bryans et al. (1998), who strongly recommended greater collaboration between professional associations and academic providers so that the appropriately designed programmes could be developed.

What Model of CPD?

In the same way that there is a range of definitions of CPD, there is also a wide range of models adopted by professional associations for monitoring and recording members' participation in CPD. A CPD model should provide a structured framework that is credible, specific and appropriate for the practice of counselling and psychotherapy. A model of CPD that is appropriate for dentists might not be suitable for psychological therapists. Further, the counsellor/therapist must be able to choose, engage in and demonstrate CPD appropriate to the context, scope and level of his or her practice. Where a professional association provides a model for CPD it should give clear guidance of what is required, why it is required and how the plan and record should be structured. However, sufficient flexibility for individuals to express their own needs must be built into that structure.

Although professional associations set standards for the education, training and professional conduct of their members, each association has its individual model for monitoring CPD. Professional associations struggle with challenging questions regarding the development of an appropriate model for CPD. For example:

- How does the professional association or regulatory body know that the activity undertaken will offer appropriate and relevant change or improvement of standards of practice?
- Does the requirement by the employer to undertake specified training deny individuals the opportunity to take full responsibility for their personal and professional development?
- Will the requirement to plan, document and evidence CPD involve individuals in unreasonable additional work when reflection is already an essential component of practice?
- How will activities be validated when individuals all learn differently – some being essentially active and others passive?
- How can all CPD be verified?
- Can e-learning qualify as valid CPD?

Professional associations seeking to develop a model for their members to use in order to demonstrate their continuing self-development could begin to design their requirements based on the idea of a SMART model for CPD. This focuses on the essential ingredients necessary. A robust model will require the written portfolio containing evidence of CPD to be:

- *Specific*. This means that the CPD programme should be planned and targeted to achieve specific outcomes. These outcomes might be the needs of the individual or the needs of the employer, or might reflect the developments in the field.

- *Monitored*. This suggests that the activities must be monitored by an external provider, verifier or regulator. It is essential that the CPD activities be subject to reflection by the individual in order to monitor the effectiveness of the learning and the appropriateness of the activity.
- *Achievable*. CPD plans must contain activities that are financially, academically and emotionally within the scope of the individual's ability. The amount of evidence required by the validating organisation must also be sensitive to the demands of busy practitioners.
- *Relevant*. CPD must above all be relevant to the current context and level of practice and also inform future improvement of practice.
- *Timed*. All CPD programmes must set boundaries of time in which a prescribed amount of CPD should be completed. This level should be the minimum suggested in order to ensure that practitioners are taking stock of present knowledge, skills and attitudes and considering what is necessary to move them forward effectively.

What Constitutes CPD?

Michael Eraut (1994), like Gardner (1978), differentiates between continuing professional education (CPE) and continuing professional development. He suggests that the former refers to 'formally organised conferences, course or educational events rather than work-based learning whereas the term "Continuing Professional Development" refers to both'.

Continuing professional activities are intended to improve and maintain competence following approved qualification. It is therefore a continuous learning process that is not restricted to learning in a classroom. Any activity can be relevant; the deciding factor is whether the activity contributes to the person performing as a better professional. The only effective CPD is outcome-based, which means that the maintenance of professional standards must be the guiding principle; any other criterion does a disservice to the ideal of professionalism. Moore and Rosenblum (1970) referred to a 'service orientation' that involves three norms: rules of competence, rules of conscientious performance and rules of service. CPD should provide learning in one or more of these three norms.

CPD activities may include lectures, seminars, workshops, distance learning, conferences, focused staff training events, in-house professional group meetings, project development, research for presentation or publication or personal development activities, assisting and supporting others and academic studies. Where possible, organised events will indicate the related number of approved professional CPD hours. However, as indicated above, the value of CPD is more importantly related to the learning outcomes achieved by the individual than the approved number of CPD hours. The individual, and not the professional association, needs to decide whether a CPD undertaking is relevant or not. The crucial question to ask is whether the effectiveness of the experience is reflected in the development of personal qualities and professional capabilities. Todd (1987) is clear that there are two criteria by which CPD can be judged

- learning has to have occurred;
- learning has to have benefited professional standards.

The HPC provides examples of context specific activities. These are indicated in Table 11.1. All these levels of practice might occur in the context of primary health care provision and no level of professional function is excused the responsibility of including CPD as a part of its self-development programme.

In addition to the above, CPD activities can include:

1 On-the-job learning: specific activities that add to the skills

TABLE 11.1
HPC examples of context-specific CPD activity

Practice	Attendance at a short course on new legislation impacting on practice
	Critical appraisal of a journal article with a group of peers
	In-service presentation to colleagues on a new technique
Education	Membership of learning and teaching committee
	Reviewer for a professional journal
	Undertaking a study for formal teaching award
	Undertaking formal presentations and teaching
Management	Member of a national occupational group for managers
	Undertake study of management modules
	Supporting the development and implementation of a national or local policy
Research	Conference presentation
	Member of local ethics research committee
	Referee of articles for scientific/vocational journal

Source: HPC CPD consultation document, p. 8.

and knowledge of the practitioner, e.g. monitored application of different interventions.

2 Private reading and study, to facilitate provision of information and instruction of colleagues, thus informing your own capability.
3 In-house conferences, workshops, seminars etc.
4 Focused professional group meetings.
5 Academic studies, including vocational qualifications, e.g. study of new approaches to psychological therapy, management of professionals delivering psychological therapy, ethical or legal issues relating to practice, use of technology relating to psychological practice, such as IT/computing, health and safety of practitioners or clients, delivery of psychological therapy involving use of other languages, such as via the use of interpreters or communicators.
6 Relevant professional institutional committee work.
7 Reviewing, writing and publishing of papers and articles.

8 Occasional lecturing, involving the development of subject material that enhances one's own proficiency.
9 Distance learning, with or without certification of that study.

The onus is on the individual to demonstrate that the chosen CPD activities are valid; in other words, that they are of real value to personal and professional development. The range of suggestions above, while relevant to organisational demands, need also to be taken into consideration if you are independently organising and planning your own CPD. Moon (1999, p. 106) states: 'whether learning is meaningful or not can only be judged by the learner because meaningfulness is an expression of the relationship between the material of learning and the learner's existing understandings'.

We all learn in different ways, and although there is an endless range of events that could contribute towards a learning experience, some activities are more effective and economically of better value than others. Considerable research has provided evidence of a range of learning styles and models for learning. It is therefore important to plan your CPD with this in mind so that you choose learning activities that will enable you to utilise your particular preferred learning strategy.

Learning Styles

The subject of learning styles and the search for effective methods of teaching and learning has attracted considerable research. Honey and Mumford (1986) and Loucks-Horsley et al. (1987) suggest that there are essentially four main learning styles: investigation, assimilation, reflection and participation. These findings have influenced the practice of teaching so that best practice includes the ability to deliver lessons in a range of styles in order to facilitate learning by all learners.

Schön (1983), Boyd and Fales (1983), Steinaker and Bell (1979) and Moon (1999) have acknowledged the value of self-reflection as a method of monitoring and improving practice and performance. Self-reflection can take many forms. Fundamental to the effectiveness of the activity is to consider current role, practice or learning activity in relation to desired or improved outcome.

Reflection can take different forms but reflection is generally taken to refer to a process involving 'complicated mental processing' (Dewey, 1933). The resulting learning emerges from an amalgamation of previous understandings with new knowledge or skills and is represented by new actions; for example, different or enhanced interventions, thought processes or writing. The reflective process is also referred to as a style of learning typified by the ability to make well considered decisions following a process of active review (Honey and Mumford, 1986). Schön, in his writing about the reflective practitioner, considers the process of reflection to be essential in order to learn from experiential knowledge.

Gibbs (1988) described an experiential reflective learning cycle:

Description: what happened?
Feelings: what were you thinking and feeling?
Evaluation: what was good and what was bad?
Analysis: what sense can you make of the situation?
Conclusion: what else could you have done?
Action plan: if it occurs again, what would you do?

Planning Your CPD

Professional associations and, by implication, their members, by adopting a requirement for CPD, demonstrate commitment to the maintenance of professional competence. This suggests that a plan is required of each individual member, who should show a methodical approach to scheduling relevant CPD so that the overall effect includes the expansion of knowledge and skills as well as the growth of personal attributes.

Megginson (1994) suggests five categories of the self that direct our professional development: our spirit, physical self, intellect, career and emotion. Megginson suggests an interesting way of thinking about our goals. For example, we could develop goals that emerge from identifying a 'career metaphor and deciding what to do about it'. Todd (1987) too identifies three areas to focus on when analysing learning needs:

- competence or what the practitioner knows;
- performance or what the practitioner does;
- effectiveness or what the practitioner achieves.

An analysis of these factors will inform a CPD plan but the plan must be developed in relation to future professional needs and interests. Anna Craft (2000, p. 49) makes reference to Gibbs and Murphy (1994), who explored learning and motivation in students and found that 'learners need to be able to develop ownership and relevance in their learning'.

The theme of working closely with what is important to us rather than what is urgent is again reinforced by Covey (1989). He suggests that to maximise effectiveness we need to focus on what is important and not on what is urgent. In this way we prepare for the future and are equipped to respond to changes from an informed position.

An individual CPD plan should be the principal focus for defining and recording personal professional development needs and achievements. Planning CPD will therefore be an annual activity that will require time and earnest attention. The CPD plan is an outcome of an analysis of current and future personal and professional needs. It is helpful, therefore, to involve a colleague, supervisor or work-based mentor in discussions about current and anticipated needs. The plan should show how the individual's needs relate to actual CPD activity and also should take into consideration developments in response to changing roles or emerging evidence-based clinical recommendations.

CPD must serve the employer's needs as well as the individual's own developmental needs. Each will have different goals. The goals of both the employer and the individual must be considered in the CPD planning process. The first step is to establish clear goals and decide on how those will be achieved and in what time frame. There are seven questions that individuals can ask themselves in the planning process to help to formulate effective action plans:

- What do I want to achieve?
- What do I need to do in order to ensure continued effective application of my skills and knowledge?
- What do I need to do in order to ensure that I am cognisant of current developments in my profession?
- What do I need to do in order to develop new skills and knowledge?
- What do I need to do in order to ensure my readiness and availability to practise?
- What is my priority?
- How will I know that CPD activities have been effective?

The answers to these questions will guide the structure of the CPD plan, which should be reviewed annually, although it may cover a period of more than one year.

Table 11.2 is an example of a Continuing Professional Development Plan developed by a newly qualified counsellor working in Primary Care Practice.

Table 11.2
Example professional development plan

Name: I. M. Dependable	Relevant CPD Period: January 2004–January 2005	Date:
What do I want to achieve?		
To achieve sufficient expertise to work as a senior counselling practitioner in a primary care setting.		April 2005
What do I need to do in order to ensure my continued effective application of my skills and knowledge?		
In order to establish my CPD needs I chose to: Spend one of my supervision sessions to discuss aspects of my clinical work that might benefit from enhanced understanding. The particular aspect identified was the need to have greater understanding of the relationship between body and mind as manifested in clients' stories.		January 2004
Discuss the possibility of promotion with my employer and agree that insight into the process of assessment in the Emergency Assessment Unit would be helpful.		February 2004
Increase my CBT skills and knowledge. The outcome of the NICE guidelines suggested to me that I should be more aware of CBT methodology and I realised that this was becoming a more recognised approach to working with some client issues.		ASAP
What do I need to do in order to ensure that I am cognisant of current developments in my profession?		
I will set aside time to read professional publications on a monthly basis.		1 hour monthly
I will reflect on the learning from the work-based group that I have joined to discuss current issues related to our work. This group meets every three months.		3 hours quarterly

What do I need to do in order to develop new skills and knowledge?	
Having identified what I need and the areas that I would like to improve, I prioritised these and realised that the understanding of the Emergency Assessment Process was essential for improving the efficacy of my referral skills. Action agreed with my employer: to contact and visit the Emergency Assessment Unit for one morning. This would take three hours.	April 2004
The second task would have to be becoming skilled and knowledgeable about CBT. Action: my research indicated that the most appropriate training would begin in September 2004 and would involve five weekends over a period of 6 months.	September 2004
Third task: to increase knowledge of somatisation Action: enrol for a forthcoming conference.	November 2004
In the interim I would find publications on somatisation and discuss the readings with my supervisor and with colleagues at our quarterly meetings.	Ongoing
What do I need to do in order to ensure my readiness and availability to practise?	
In order to deal with the demands of work and family I participate in a regular exercise programme but in addition I take time out for an annual three-day retreat.	August 2004
How will I know that CPD activities have been effective?	
I will keep a reflective record of activities.	Ongoing

Accessing Continuing Professional Development

Professional associations need to take the responsibility to engage new members in CPD so that the process becomes part of the culture of professional practice. They must make clear statements about the aims and benefits so that members understand the purpose and therefore more readily engage with the practice of CPD. Professional associations must also be a source of reference for valid and up-to-date CPD activities and should provide CPD events as a part of their ongoing activities.

Employers have some responsibility for enabling the development and maintenance of CPD schemes as an essential part of their appraisal system. A plan and record completed for the employee's professional association will provide adequate evidence for the employer, whether that is the primary care trust, the community mental health trust or a private agency managing the delivery of psychological therapies in the community.

Sources of CPD include qualifications approved on the National Qualifications Framework and its successor, the Framework for Achievement (FfA).[1] Training that enhances the capabilities of the practitioner following initial qualification as a practitioner is offered by further education colleges, private providers and higher education institutions.

Training leading to qualifications at level 5 or above, which will prepare counsellors for work in the primary care sector, will be considered valid CPD for those who have already achieved practitioner status. Two such courses are the CPCAB Level 5 Diploma in Psychotherapeutic Counselling, with the descriptor 'Working in Health Care Settings', and 'Primary Care Counsellors' offered by the Tavistock and Portman NHS Trust. Universities also offer formal academic qualifications that can be taken as individual modules or full degree qualifications. Counsellors and Psychotherapists in Primary Care also offers a programme of CPD, which can be accessed via the website www.cpc-online.co.uk. The programme includes a range of one-day workshops on subjects relevant to counsellors in primary care.

Recording Your CPD

Records of CPD should be retained on an ongoing basis as evidence of completion, achievement and learning. Whichever way it is recorded, a CPD record should:

- show a systematic plan for at least one year;
- document the activities that have helped to increase fitness to practice or efficiency, including the date, type of activity and duration;
- include reflection on the benefits of each activity in relation to your individual and/or organisation's prioritised needs;
- ideally include how the learning will impact on future practice.

It is important to reflect on the CPD event because this constitutes a form of activity in relation to the process of learning. Revans (1998) suggests that 'there can be no learning without action and no (sober and deliberate) action without learning'. Active involvement in learning is essential to the learning process: passively participating in an event, despite the fact that the event might carry recognised CPD hours, does not ensure effective learning. Reflection is a method of actively participating in the process of learning and can include comment on what happened, what impact the event had on you, what ideas or insights you gained from the event, what the outcome was of sharing your learning with others, how effective the skills and knowledge were when you implemented them, what you felt about the event and what action you might take or changes you might propose in relation to the event. The recording of and reflection on the process and outcomes of CPD is fundamental to the implementation of learning from events and is critical for the development of our skills, knowledge and qualities.

Effective reflective practice is the cornerstone of effective clinical practice. Schön (1983) notes that 'Reflection upon action is the process of considering events afterwards so that practice can effectively be enhanced.' He even refers to reflection in action as 'the Hawk in your mind'. That is not unlike the emphasis that Kolb (1984) places on the experiential stage of learning, i.e. learning from reflecting on experience.

Table 11.3 is an example of a CPD record for one year kept by a newly qualified counsellor in a primary care practice.

Conclusion

John Ferguson (1970) reflects on the life of Socrates and reports that: 'Socrates in his wisdom made an assumption of his own ignorance'. It is clear that CPD is more than attendance at courses or prescribed activities. CPD embraces any learning activity that is relevant to the development of competencies and qualities related to the individual's professional practice and that improves that practice.

Professional associations have, according to the NHS White Paper 1997, greater self-regulatory responsibilities. This responsibility begins with the entry training standard and extends through the professional life of its members. They must work towards greater clarity as to what constitutes good practice in relation to CPD. The response to this concern will emerge from the creation of a collaborative relationship between the professional associations in which they exchange examples of good practice from the perspective of the association and from the perspective of its members. The professional associations must now fully accept their part in the responsible care of the public by ensuring that their members undertake appropriate and fruitful CPD. Individual members take guidance from the professional associations' policies and procedures on CPD. They must therefore give members clear information about what is needed and why it is needed: for example, 'to ensure continued employability'.

The interface of the social, physical and psychological aspects of

TABLE 11.3
Example record of continuous professional development

Name: I. M. Dependable | *Relevant CPD period: January 2004 to January 2005*

Objective	*Mode of CPD*	*Date completed*	*Hours involved*	*Reflection on CPD event*	*Comments*
To maintain currency and update knowledge	Read professional publications	Ongoing	This activity is expected and is not regarded as formal CPD		
To maintain currency and update knowledge	Work-based group meeting to discuss current issues	January 2004	12 hours	Colleague raised difficulty of maintaining boundaries in her clinical work in a primary care unit where other non-medical therapists also work. I had been uneasy about how to respond to some of the questions I had been asked by staff in the unit. This discussion was helpful in clarifying the communication pathways and processes necessary for resolving such issues and my responsibility for sharing relevant clinical information between members of the primary care team.	

Name: I. M. Dependable *Relevant CPD period: January 2004 to January 2005*

Objective	*Mode of CPD*	*Date completed*	*Hours involved*	*Reflection on CPD event*	*Comments*
		April 2004		Discussed the question of the value of brief therapy. We addressed the question of how brief is brief and when it would be appropriate to extend the definition of 'brief' to 20 or more sessions. I realised that I was not alone in this struggle. There were situations when there could be some flexibility in this ruling and I gained clearer understanding of this and the other options available to me.	
		July 2004		This was taken over by a presentation on child protection. I found this particularly reassuring because I learned that the Child and Family Services provided a confidential consultation service for health workers to discuss child protection issues, which is particularly useful in marginal cases.	
		October 2004		I will present my paper on somatisation at this session.	
To increase understanding of the Emergency Assessment Process	Visit the NHS Emergency Assessment Unit for one morning	25 April 2004	3 hours	Absolutely invaluable. I gained insight into how clients sometimes turned up on my list despite having had consultation with the hospital psychiatrist. I am now clearer about some referral issues and now know that I can also provide clients with information about this service.	Remember to take the experience of the client's visit to the EAU into consider-ation in my work.

To become skilled and knowledgeable about CBT	Attend training course	September 2004 to February 2005	September to January Total 56 hours	Not yet done	
To increase knowledge of somatisation	Enrol for a forthcoming one-day conference	November 2004	5 hours	Not yet done	
	Read publications on somatisation and produce a paper for discussion with my supervisor and with colleagues at our quarterly meetings	August, 2 days	14 hours	My focused reading is really interesting and has become personally relevant. I am already making use of my understanding; for example, in the case of diabetics who do not conform to the recommended treatment regime. I am able to empathise with clients'/patients' resistance to ownership of the disease. Not being medically trained I used to find diabetic clients' resistance to their prescribed care plan quite frustrating.	Look up diabetes on the Internet.
To increase self-awareness of personal psychological well-being	Annual retreat	August 3 days	12 hours	A well needed break. My recent reading on the subject of somatisation really began to make more sense to me over these three days. I had been exhausted and put that down to other causes. Now I realise that I was mentally fatigued. I needed to stop to allow body and mind energy to be synchronised and to be aware of my lack of synchrony.	Think about how I can take time out more frequently to do nothing.
			Total 102 hours		

life is ever present in the caseload of therapists and counsellors working in the primary care setting. The relationship between these aspects and the presenting concerns of clients is complex and presents the counsellor with the challenge of working empathically with the whole person and the broader external systems that impact on that very specific and unique alliance. The totality of the relationship between the parts of this picture provides a startling image of the mantle of professional responsibility that individual counsellors hold for their practice. The responsibility for continued effectiveness of practitioners must, however, be jointly shared by the professional association, the practitioner and the employer.

Within the context of rapid and continuing social and demographic change, it is in the interest of everyone concerned with the promotion and enhancement of mental health to work towards reducing what we do not know and understand and to improve our potential to work effectively with what we do know.

Note

1 The FfA is a framework for recognising achievements approved by the regulators, the QCA in England. ACCAC for Wales and CCEA in Scotland have similar frameworks.

References

Boyd, E. and Fales, A. (1983) Reflective learning: key to learning from experience. *Journal of Human Psychology*, 23, 94–117.

Bryans, P., Gormley, N., Stalker, B. and Williamson, B. (1998) From collusion to dialogue: universities and continuing professional development. *Continuing Professional Development Journal*, 1, 120–8.

Covey, S. R. (1989) *The Seven Habits of Highly Effective People*. London: Franklin Covey Co.

Eraut, M. (1994) *Developing Professional Knowledge and Competence*. London: Falmer Press.

Ferguson, J. (1970) *Socrates: A Source Book*. Milton Keynes: Open University Press.

Freidman, A., Davis, K., Durkin, C. and Phillips, M. (2000) *Continuing Professional Development in the UK: Policies and Programmes*. London: PARN.

Gardner, R. (1978) *Policy on Continuing Education: A Report with Recommendations for Action*. York: University of York.

Honey, P. and Mumford, A. (1986). *The Manual of Learning Styles*. Maidenhead: Peter Honey and Alan Mumford.

Kolb, D. A. (1984) *Experiential Learning: Experience as a Source of Learning and Development*. Englewood Cliffs, NJ: Prentice Hall.

Loucks-Horsley, S., Arbuckle, M., Dubea, C., Harding, C., Murray, L. and Williams, M. (1987) *Continuing to Learn: A Guide Book for Teacher Development*. Andover: Regional Laboratory for Educational Improvement of the Northeast and Islands and National Staff Development Council.

Megginson, D. and Whitaker, V. (2003) *Continuing Professional Development*. London: CIPD.

Moon, J. A. (1999) *Reflection in Learning and Professional Development*. London: Kogan Page.

Moore, W. E. and Rosenblum, G. W. (1970) *The Professions: Roles and Rules*. New York: Russell Sage Foundation.

Revans, R. (1998) *ABC of Action Learning*. London: Lemos and Crane.

Schön, D. A. (1983) *The Reflective Practitioner: How Professionals Think in Action*. New York: Basic Books.

Steinaker, N. W. and Bell, M. R. (1979) *The Experiential Taxonomy*. New York: Academic Press.

Todd, F. (ed.) (1987) *Planning Continuing Professional Development*. London: Croom Helm.

Vaughan, P. (1991) *Maintaining Professional Competence: A Survey of the Role of Professional Bodies in the Development of Credit-bearing CPD Courses*. Hull: University of Hull.

Welsh, L. and Woodward, P. (1989) *Continuing Professional Development: Towards a National Strategy*. Glasgow: Planning Exchange.

Part III

The Role Sets and Relationships between Roles in Counselling in Primary Care

CHAPTER TWELVE

Fitness to Practise: Selection for Primary Care

Choosing and Supporting the Competent Practitioners: A Service Manager's View

Antonia Murphy

Introduction

As has already been documented by a number of the authors in this book, counselling was first introduced as a clinical initiative in a few GP surgeries in the late 1970s. Its incorporation as part of the range of services available in primary care teams gradually increased through the 1980s and mushroomed in the 1990s. Prior to the introduction of primary care commissioning under the auspices of the new primary care groups/trusts in 2001 there were counsellors in approximately 50 per cent of GP surgeries nationally. Primary care counselling has developed from a loose structure of individual counsellors and some managed services to the position today of approximately 80 per cent of primary care trusts having a managed primary care counselling service in place.

These early counsellors or psychotherapists were traditionally trained in open-ended counselling and in a number of different core theoretical orientations. They were often the first counsellor to work in a particular surgery and had as such a very steep learning curve. They had to learn to work to a limited number of sessions, and with an incredibly wide spectrum of clients with a variety of presenting issues within a medical setting with its own distinct paradigm.

As such it could be argued that a new profession has emerged during this evolution – that of the primary care counsellor. These days this title could be rightly extended to that of the NHS psychological therapist – the practitioner now so familiar in the NHS who provides therapeutic assessment and intervention to patients with a wide range of mental health problems at their first point of access, namely primary care.

With the rise of this new professional comes the concomitant need for definition, standard setting and professional and clinical governance. From this basis selection against agreed criteria is relatively straightforward. As we have noted already, counselling and psychotherapy are unregulated at present, and while there are lead professional bodies that set their own standards, there are no national statutory guidelines in place. It is therefore essential for the profession, for safety and for good practice within the health service that criteria and selection for counsellors and psychological therapists are in place. If sound selection can take place until the establishment of regulatory standards and in parallel to their agreement then regulation will be a far easier task in the future.

However, the profession is not unanimous in its approach to training or even in its agreement over standards. As this book details, the Counselling and Psychotherapy Forum for Primary Care, with membership from all the lead organisations, was formed to set minimum standards (Appendix 2) specifically for primary care counsellors and psychotherapists, which are detailed and expanded on throughout this book. This is a good start for a profession that has many representative bodies with various introductions into the NHS. The agreed specification for counsellors working in the NHS is given in Appendix 3.

It is against this backdrop that I want to explore in more detail the need for, definition of, and criteria for selection into the profession of psychological therapy and into work within the NHS.

Why Selection?

We can choose to train to become competent specialists in all sorts of realms and fields of work. In so doing we aim if we can to be consistent, good or good enough and safe. Counselling is no different in this respect from other professions. Criteria are agreed and candidates are chosen against these criteria and trained accordingly to achieve qualification. In this way selection is a counterpart to training and in the context of the counselling profession is essential to successful completion of training and to productive, effective and efficacious work thereafter. However, because of the clinical nature of counselling work and because the therapeutic relationship is the bedrock of the work, selection for counselling is a question not just of weighing up the academic or vocational merit of applicants but also of assessing their psychological and personal suitability. In the NHS, where the work of counselling takes place in a much more complex setting, owing to the multidisciplinary nature of the frame, selection of counsellors who can hold their own psychological, professional and personal boundaries is essential.

The arguments for careful and knowledgeable selection and suitability for NHS work are not just based on those that we in the profession would expect to be upheld but are allied to the NHS itself. Following a radical reframing of primary care health services, commissioning of clinical services including psychological therapies is now being driven from within the primary care organisations. Clinical governance is the new mission, central to the government's reforms. This spells out that all services are to be delivered within standards set via professional self-regulation thus:

> Clinical governance and life long learning will help instil quality at a local level throughout commissioning. This places services such as counselling hitherto at the mercy of individual innovative practices or Trusts much more centre stage and much more under scrutiny. The government's National Institute of Clinical Governance (NICE) will be instrumental in ensuring the NHS. Both are founded on the principle that health professionals must be responsible and accountable for their own practice. (DoH, 2000, p. 43)

Clinical governance will provide: 'A framework through which NHS organisations are accountable for continuously improving the quality of their services and safeguarding high standards of care by creating an environment in which excellence in clinical care will flourish' (Donaldson, 1998).

The employment of counsellors in the haphazard and ad hoc forms of counselling's early origins in the NHS certainly led to the development of much creative and innovative practice in GP surgeries. However, it also led to inconsistent provision and sometimes unethical and exploitative arrangements between counsellor and employer. At times trainee or unqualified counsellors have been working unsupported and unpaid in surgeries without adequate supervision, managerial support or experience of the setting. Some have argued that too much management – referral protocols, time limits, selection criteria – may well diminish variation, individuality and creativity in the counselling work. But the aim of creating improved and well defined conditions for counsellors working in the NHS is to clip their wings but to provide them with a safer frame within which they can work.

Under the newly constituted primary care organisations counselling in primary care has to meet the standards of clinical governance. Professional NHS counselling can now use this momentum to set and maintain standards of excellence so that good quality, well managed counselling can be offered through every PCG/PCT in the country. As such, selection of counsellors to work in this setting takes place at three stages:

1 At the outset and prior to any generic training (see all the chapters in Part II).
2 At the next stage of entry into an NHS-specific training and/or placement.
3 Again at interview for NHS posts at all levels.

In this way we parallel other NHS professions, such as nursing or clinical psychology, having professional standards, agreed entry training and entry criteria, subsequent professional qualification and career development through further training and job experience. From this follows professional respect from medical colleagues, professional accountability, which is sanctioned and safeguarded, and finally professional development and a career trajectory for counsellors and psychotherapists.

Selection for the characteristics of self-discipline, rigour and integrity is required alongside selection for academic and intellectual abilities, so that the individual ability of the practitioner can develop safely and thoughtfully. Such selection is part of the safe bedrock of a profession from which highly specialised and experienced clinicians who are much needed in the NHS can work competently and flexibly but most importantly safely within their own clinical and personal limits. Knowing these limits is tantamount to safe and best practice.

That Special Person!

Elsewhere in this book we consider the person specification and minimum training standard as agreed within the Forum for entry into the profession. The selection process required for initial counselling training is also explored in Chapter Four. Thus I want to focus in this section on the detail required of a counsellor in the NHS so that we know the criteria against which selection needs to take place at the outset of generic training, on application for a trainee placement in the NHS and finally on application to work in the NHS.

A counsellor entering the NHS at Band 5 (see Agenda for Change job profiles, Appendix 7), which is the newly qualified level, needs to have completed generic training to at least degree level or degree level diploma over a period of three years. This training would include:

- study of the theory and practice of counselling from assessment to termination;
- understanding of human development, psychopathology, sexuality, ethics and research;
- training in counselling techniques;
- supervised practice of counselling in a managed placement, with the initial placement in a generic setting of at least 100 hours before placement in NHS;
- a knowledge of a range of counselling and psychotherapeutic approaches to enable an awareness of differing treatment options;
- training in recognition of serious mental illness;
- training in assessment skills to ensure counselling is not offered inappropriately to clients;
- training in management of the appropriate therapeutic intervention for each client;
- knowledge of relevant legal issues pertaining to counselling work;
- the ability to recognise when the practitioner should seek other professional advice;
- knowledge of relevant ethical frameworks for practice.

Moreover, the counsellor will be required to have covered some specialist modules relevant to NHS and medical settings and undertaken a placement in an NHA setting. Such further specialist coverage could be in the following areas:

- knowledge of psychotropic medication and its relevance to client work;

- awareness of the nature of the dynamics of groups and the impact of the organisation on the therapeutic frame;
- somatisation – mind and body;
- legal and ethical issues with respect to statutory health care;
- audit, evaluation, outcome measurement;
- evidence-based practice;
- working within a time limit.

These are by no means definitive lists and their coverage will vary depending on the modality of the generic and specialist training. However, the overall list is extensive and complex – just like the work the NHS counsellor will be undertaking. As such, selection for clinicians working in the NHS must aim to discover whether the practitioner has covered these areas in his or her training and is able to think and use them as a foundation for good practice. The NHS counsellor needs a deep, robust core training, on top of which is a thorough comprehensive coverage of specialist areas relevant to NHS work. Naturally through continuing professional development (CPD) all clinicians will continue to grow in their work once in post, but it is vitally important that initial training and specific NHS training are thoroughly grounded.

Further to these specific areas of study and practice counsellors need to have undertaken personal therapy together with a managed supervised placement. Both these are additional criteria for the qualified counsellor and therefore to be considered in selection. However, the need for personal therapy as an essential part of training continues to be debated in the profession. The BACP currently specifies a requirement for practitioner self-awareness – not the same as personal therapy – whereas CPC specifies a minimum of 40 hours of personal therapy. The new UKCP psychotherapeutic section specifies a minimum of 50 hours of personal therapy. My own opinion is that there is an imperative for personal therapy as part of a counsellor's training because the therapeutic relationship is the mode and means to the work. Basically personal therapy is the core ingredient to counselling and psychotherapy training because it is by this means that practitioners are able to allow themselves to be available in the transference without contaminating the process. It is essential to training, not optional. Self-awareness is one of the many outcomes of therapy but it is not the sole reason for undertaking it for training purposes, although it may be more gratifying than other more challenging aspects of personal therapy.

A full professional counselling training is first and foremost a clinical training; thus it needs the clinician to be psychologically fit for the work. Selection and continual assessment for such training is based not only on academic criteria but also on psychological and personal suitability for training. To sum up what might be best achieved by a thorough training as outlined above, psychotherapeutic counsellors who go on to work in the NHS or elsewhere would be able:

- To reflect critically on the psychotherapeutic process in which they are engaged, to be psychologically aware and to know why they want to do this work, what it will entail of them and what it is for.
- To take part in their own self-reflection in relation to their work as a result of their own therapy and continuing supervision.
- To have a realistic appreciation of the value and limits of their work and of their own capabilities and to know where, whether and how to refer on. This is particularly relevant to NHS work.
- To work within their professional boundaries while recognising the benefit and challenges of others.

Thus it follows that anyone considering undertaking initial generic counselling training should judge the suitability and quality of the training regarding not only what it covers but also how well candidates are scrutinised and selected. This process needs to include all aspects of selection, including the psychological. How well the training institute covers this is a measure of the probity it exercises and therefore of its value. It is likely to be a measure of how well trained you will be as a result of completing the training process and will put you in good stead for further selection in the workplace and most importantly for being able to undertake best clinical practice.

Selecting the Person

As we have noted, the profession of counselling is still not regulated by statute (unlike dentists or doctors or nurses). However, the professional bodies for counselling in the NHS, such as CPC (Association for Counsellors and Psychotherapists in the NHS), are self-regulating and have set training standards for registration. But there is still, as such, no protection of the term counsellor. This as we know has led to confusion and difficulties in the workplace, particularly in the NHS, since many nurses and other health professionals have undertaken counselling skills training alongside their core professional training. The recent work by ENTO and QCA on the revision of the suite of counselling qualifications has teased out the difference between counselling skills and counselling as a professional. Counselling skills qualifications are at QCA level 3, while entry level to the profession as a practitioner is at QCA level 4 (see Appendix 5). It is important to be clear about the difference between fully qualified counsellors and those who may use counselling skills as a useful adjunct to their work. So one of the first steps in selection is to be clear about the person specification for the post. If it is a counselling post then only qualified counsellors are eligible to apply (see Appendix 3).

Having established that the posts for selection are counselling posts (either Agenda for Change entry level (band 5) or counsellor (band 6)), NHS managers need to be seeking counsellors who are *qualified, knowledgeable, competent, safe, reflective and mature practitioners who can work with others*. This sounds straightforward enough but contains a great deal in the detail. It might be helpful to break down such requirements into more specific terms, which could be thought of as an extended person specification.

Thus if we look at the area of *qualifications and knowledge* we are seeking someone who:

- is trained to an agreed standard (see Appendices 2 and 3);
- is grounded in a core theory of which they can demonstrate a thorough understanding;
- has specialist training in and knowledge of the NHS;
- has knowledge of mental illness and personality disorder;
- has knowledge of NHS structures and of primary care/ secondary and tertiary interfacing;
- is familiar with legal and ethical issues relevant to therapeutic work in the NHS;
- is familiar with current research and willing to participate in research studies and evaluations.

In matters of *competency, safety and best practice* we can add someone who:

- is experienced and trained in clinical assessment, time-limited work and long-term work;
- is experienced in working with a range of complex cases from diverse backgrounds and ages;
- has undertaken personal therapy (see above) and is in ongoing supervision with a recognised supervisor with NHS knowledge and expertise;
- works to a code of ethical practice relevant to the NHS;
- would keep notes and records in line with practice/NHS requirements;
- has an expectation of value – is graded and paid in line with Agenda for Change and on the correct banding for training, experience and job specification;
- is organised and professional (i.e. can undertake audits and evaluations etc.);

- is committed to relevant CPD on a yearly basis (30 hours a year minimum);
- has an awareness of diversity issues and their impact on the counselling relationship.

In terms of being able *to work with others* we will be seeking those who:

- can make good working relationships with colleagues – can be part of a team as well as hold professional and personal boundaries;
- are confident and competent to discuss clinical matters with a range of health professionals;
- are able to attend service meetings and contribute to development of the service in relation to joined up mental health planning (i.e. doesn't just want to see patients).

Note also that counsellors have usually worked in a previous profession and as such may undertake training and selection for posts at a later stage in life. As such much of their earlier experience in life and work contributes to their suitability for this work and can be taken into consideration. Foster and Murphy (2005) state that:

> Many counsellors have worked extensively in a previous profession for a number of years, not necessarily in a related field. All the competencies and experience they have gained elsewhere help them attend with the kind of integrity and containment required for the job. It is tremendously important that the psychological therapist working in the NHS is experienced and competent to work with a very wide range of patients, in a mixed provision of depth work. . . . If you are looking to recruit counsellors to work in primary care you want someone who:
>
> - is initially very well trained and very familiar with her own core theory

- is confident enough to know how to do her work and to know her limitations
- can seek the help and support of others as well as be available to offer it
- is thirsty for knowledge and keen to grow in experience
- can make good relationships.

(Foster and Murphy, 2005)

The Selection Process

The task of selection begins at recruitment. Given this, it is as well to cover as many bases as possible in terms of advertising when recruiting, while bearing in mind that there will be constraints of cost and time. At the same time it is important to design a selection and interview process that will be fair but will also allow selection on the basis of what is being sought, as described in the sections above.

Thus a service manager wanting to recruit counsellors into the NHS needs to:

- Advertise widely stating the terms of the job; the entry qualifications; the level and A4C banding of the post; and provide a job specification on application.
- Establish criteria for short listing according to the person specification.
- Set up an interview panel, preferably with a clinical expert, internal human resources and management representative.
- Ask for a short case presentation giving a brief to the candidates in advance.
- Draw up suitable questions that will reveal clinical competency, experience and knowledge of the NHS setting, as well as thorough grounding in clinical model and use of supervision, personal integrity and safe practice.
- Be even handed and try not to be influenced by one's own

clinical preferences – hence the value of others on the interview panel.
- Think about what is being sought and why – can you see this person as a member of a team of counsellors, of other health professionals, as being accessible to a broad range of people? Would you refer a patient to them?
- Choose applicants based on how they match the criteria and according to scoring.

It is useful to include an external assessor on the interview panel as well as a member of the human resource department. The process of interview is designed to get a sense of the counsellor's competency in the first place, but more than this, it is to establish that he or she will be able to work flexibly and communicate effectively within a primary care team. Remember that counsellors working in primary care need to do more than simply undertake ongoing client work. They need to be able to:

- assess clients;
- identify when the presenting problem requires a different intervention;
- establish appropriate contracts and boundaries;
- formulate an appropriate therapeutic intervention;
- establish a therapeutic relationship;
- use the therapeutic process effectively to benefit the client;
- work to an agreed ending with the client within service level limits;
- participate in collaborative work with other health professionals;
- use supervision extensively.

Any interview process needs to be carefully structured so that all these main features of the work of counsellors in primary care are considered. Counsellors who work in primary care are being selected on the basis that they are not only good clinical practitioners but also team players who are able to hold their own in what can be an extremely complex organisational setting. It is necessary to recruit counsellors into the NHS who are able to retain a certain creativity and autonomy while working within the statutory requirements of the health service.

Conclusion

It is clear that counselling in the health service has come a long way. Through newly defined career pathways and Agenda for Change bandings we now see that counselling has a place in the NHS. Counselling is now an integral part of the delivery of psychological therapies. In many places in the country counselling service managers are leaders in the development of high standard and effective therapeutic interventions in primary care that meet the mental health needs of large numbers of patient populations.

Selection according to the best standards of training and suitability plays a key part in the continuing development of primary care counselling services. The final stage of the selection process, which begins with initial training placement and continues with selection for placement, is that of selection into post. At each stage equal care needs to be taken that candidates are selected not only for their ability to perform competently or efficiently but also for their capacity to be available to their patients in a very particular way in order to facilitate the arrival, in the therapeutic dyad, at some kind of psychic truth. This particular type of work needs very particular training in order to produce clinicians with the necessary competencies, knowledge, insight, maturity and integrity. It follows that selection at any stage must be mindful of all the areas that delineate a safe counsellor clinician.

Professional counsellors working in the NHS need to be able to think and contain a great deal of anxiety and conflicting expectations. Selection for counselling in general is a complex process in itself, balancing knowledge of what can be known about applicants against what will be required of them. Selection for counsellors who are able to work within a different paradigm such as that of the medical model is even more of a challenge. In putting selection of counsellors in a central position in relation to the aim of providing consistent comprehensive counselling services in the NHS, it is hoped that the task of designing and delivering such provision is made easier. Furnishing the reader with some of the necessary detail of this process of selection will mean that a more consistent and achievable approach to counselling service design is possible.

References

Department of Health (2000) *The New NHS*. London: HMSO.

Donaldson (1998) *Organising and Delivering Psychological Therapies*. London: Department of Health.

Foster, P. J. and Murphy, A. (2005) *Psychological Therapies in Primary Care – Setting up a Managed Service*. London: Karnac.

CHAPTER THIRTEEN

Professional Liability Insurance

Protection for the Public, Protection for the Therapist

Steve Johnson

WHEN professional bodies and others set standards for training they do so to help to ensure that, as far as possible, best practice is adopted by those about to commence working in the profession and the risk of malpractice or negligence through bad practice is eliminated. This is primarily for the protection of members of the public (users of the service) but it also protects the practitioner by providing a safe, tried and tested model for practice. Application of what we learn in training and the adherence to the codes of ethics or ethical frameworks of the relevant professional body by the counsellor or psychotherapist is part of the process of *risk management* that anyone in business or acting as a professional should undertake. We need to identify and quantify the risks we are exposed to and, as far as possible, eliminate them. Risk management can only go so far and it is never possible, in the real world, to eliminate risk completely. Counsellors and psychotherapists are human and human beings make mistakes, they make errors of judgement and are, on occasion, negligent; they can (and do!) get things wrong.

In our everyday lives, we all owe a duty of care towards those that we encounter, not to cause them to suffer harm or damage by our actions or omissions. For the professional, that duty becomes more specific and the standard of care expected is more than what would be expected from just another member of the public. For counsellors and psychotherapists these standards are, mostly, enshrined in the codes of ethics and practice and/or the ethical framework. If we breach that duty of care, judged against the appropriate standards, then we are accountable for the consequences and, usually, this will mean *financially* accountable. It could, of course, also mean that we are accountable *professionally* to our professional body or other regulator under the complaints or disciplinary procedures.

When things do go wrong, the law of the land provides the mechanism for putting things right by ensuring (through the court system) that those who are in breach of their duty of care compensate those who have been injured or who have suffered loss as a result of that breach. But where does that compensation come from? That is not a primary concern for the court; if a court finds that you are responsible for injury, loss or damage it will make an award against you and *you* will have to pay; where the money comes from is, as we have said, not the concern of the court. If you don't have the cash (and which of us do, bearing in mind that we could be looking at a duty to pay compensation of many thousands of pounds?) then your assets are at risk; that's your house, your car, your savings, your livelihood!

This is where insurance might be of help, but we will come back to that. We talked earlier of risk management; we have reduced the risk as far as possible by adhering to ethical codes and frameworks and by adopting recognised best practice, but what do we do with the element of risk that inevitably remains? What we should do first is to quantify it. What are the consequences if I *do* make a mistake? How much will it cost? If all dissatisfied customers (or clients or patients or service users) could be satisfied by a simple refund of fees, then we might decide to retain the risk ourselves. Sadly, life is not that simple, and the consequences of being responsible for injury or damage to others are real, and serious. Accepting that we, probably, don't wish to retain the risk ourselves, what options do we have?

Employment

Being employed by someone else (rather than being self-employed) does not mean that you are absolved of any liability that you may have as a result of a breach of your duty of care. What it does mean (usually) is that your employer, under whose general guidance you will be working, will have vicarious liability for your acts, errors or omissions. Effectively, the employer will *also* be responsible for the consequences of any breach of professional duty committed by you, but there remains the possibility that you personally could find yourself being sued for damages either as well as, or instead of, your employer. The choice of whom to name in a legal action is that of the person bringing the claim. Usually, but not always, they will name the employer as that is where they will stand the best chance of funds being available to pay damages. Often they will name as many parties as possible in the hope that someone will have the funds (or the insurance) to pay up. Occasionally, we have seen claims brought solely against the employee, either to be vindictive or to seek revenge for perceived harm inflicted, or perhaps even because the relationship between the employee and employer is not known or not clear.

In an employer/employee relationship, it is usual for the employer to provide an indemnity to the employee and for the employee to be covered under any professional liability insurance held by the employer. If you are in any doubt as to either the intention of an employer to provide an indemnity or the insurance arrangements they have in place, then you should enquire. Be aware also that you (and they) will only be covered by any insurance policy they may have up to its limit of indemnity and you should, as far as you can, satisfy yourself that this limit is adequate. In addition, where you are relying on someone else's insurance policy to protect you, you are also reliant on them complying with the terms and conditions of that policy. This is an important point, particularly in relation to notification to the insurers, in a timely manner, of any circumstances that could give rise to a claim being made. Similar considerations apply if you are working as a volunteer or on a supervised placement, in that you should check whether you are provided with an indemnity and/ or covered under an insurance policy arranged by the 'employer'. If necessary you should consider arranging a policy to provide yourself with the protection you need (see 'Insurance' below).

In most cases where you are working as an associate or a self-employed sub-contractor and in some cases where you are a volunteer or on placement, you will be expected to arrange your own insurance. This will usually be made clear (but not always) in the terms of the contract between you.

Contract

It is possible to use contract terms as a risk transfer mechanism, a means of transferring risk to others but only to a limited extent. While a disclaimer notice (or contract term) that 'no liability can be accepted for loss of or damage to personal belongings left in the waiting room, however caused' may be OK, UK law does not permit us to contract out of liability for death or injury (including mental injury) caused by our negligence, so a disclaimer that 'all counselling is undertaken at your own risk' would not work, and would probably not be good for business or for client confidence! All contract terms that attempt to restrict liability must be reasonable, particularly where you might be deemed to be the party in the stronger position when you are using a standard form. We should also be aware of contracts as a means of transferring risk from others to us. Please be sure to read and understand any contract you may be asked to sign *before* you sign it, be aware of any additional risks that the contract might be trying to impose and, if necessary, discuss these risks with your insurers to make sure your policy covers them. Most policies do provide cover for liability assumed under contract, in most circumstances; but, if you are unsure, please do check.

Insurance

This brings us nicely on to insurance. Insurance is a risk transfer mechanism that works by pooling risks. Each participant in the pool pays an annual premium that has been calculated by the insurers, using their knowledge and experience of the market sector, to provide sufficient funds for the pool to meet all of its liabilities (claims), cover expenses and running costs and provide a return on the capital invested by the insurer (profit). Any surplus or deficit would contribute to, or be subsidised from, the reserves of the insurer.

If we are transferring the risk to the insurer (by purchasing a policy from them), why all the emphasis on risk management and standards? Surely that becomes their problem? Well, the answer is yes and no. Remember that it is only the *residual* risk that is transferred, and the lesser that residual risk, the smaller will be the risk transfer premium. A profession that has sound standards for the training of its students and codes of ethics or ethical frameworks that are understood and followed by its members is more likely to persuade an insurer (or at least an insurer that understands the profession) that the risks are low, and therefore so should be the premiums.

Insurers will always feel more at ease when they understand the risks that they take on. This is why certain insurers tend to specialise in different market sectors and is one of the reasons why I have been happy to participate in and contribute in some small way to the various forum meetings looking into and helping to set standards in training for counsellors and psychotherapists and why it has been a pleasure contributing to this book.

Professional liability insurance is about protection:

- protection of the public (service users) by making sure that, when things do go wrong, funds *are* available to meet compensation claims;
- protection for you, the professional, not only by providing funds to meet valid compensation claims but also in defending yourself against spurious or ill founded claims.

To that degree, insurers and those looking to set and raise standards in the profession share a commonality of purpose.

CHAPTER FOURTEEN

Opportunity or Threat? What Is Happening to Psychological Therapies in the NHS? A View of Primary Care as New Relationships Emerge

Jane Rosoman

PSYCHOLOGICAL therapies have a substantial contribution to make to primary care and this is increasingly recognised. Michael Balint (1957) recognised the psychological issues presented in primary care 50 years ago and suggested psychotherapy had a place there. Patients have recognised the need and consistently asked for more resources for counselling and psychotherapy to be made available. Doctors have long recognised the value of talking treatments to complement all the other treatments available in primary care. Yet recognition by policy-makers and the necessary resources have been slow to follow. Massive changes are under way and this chapter describes some of the recent initiatives that form a backdrop to the development of mental health services in primary care. The focus of the chapter is to explain the wider systems that may help or hinder the development of psychological therapies. The final section considers the impact of current developments on the provision of services and what practitioners, managers and commissioners need to consider, as ways of interpreting the guidelines and different models of practice emerge.

Transitions are always interesting and stressful. Therapists know that in patients' lives the negotiation of transitions is frequently the catalyst for seeking help. The usual ways of dealing with things no longer work and the markers that give meaning and security are no longer relevant or have disappeared altogether, leading to feelings of not coping and disorientation. Change and transition has become a necessary and problematic way of life for the NHS and it is the employees who may feel stressed, disoriented and not able to cope. Yet we therapists also know that it is through negotiating chaotic and difficult times that creative solutions emerge, leading to more satisfying ways of living. Those of us with systemic leanings no longer believe that these changes can be managed in their entirety because the context is always in flux. The delivery of health care has become a complex business, and complexity theory and systemic thinking have a very different way of seeing things that still needs time to gain currency in the wider world. Yet we have to look for possibilities and opportunities to develop good practice as wave after wave of new initiatives break over us. We have sufficient grounding in our professional practice to make headway in these uncertain times because uncertainty is the business of our everyday work as counsellors and therapists.

It is no longer possible for counsellors and psychotherapists in primary care to focus solely on the relationship with the patient. The move to a managed service has brought changes to practice in what is still an unregulated profession. It is important that counsellors, managers and trainers understand the context in which the work is undertaken. With this in mind, the following section reviews current directives for NHS organisations.

Government Initiatives

This section highlights a few key documents but does not claim to be a comprehensive review. The modernisation programme, begun in 1997 with the publication of *The New NHS: Modern, Dependable,* set the scene for all subsequent directives by outlining how all NHS organisations are accountable for quality, monitoring and the improvement in care. By 2004, developments had led to the setting up of the Healthcare Commission (Health and Social Care Act 2003), which set seven core standards against which health care organisations must measure themselves and submit an annual declaration. These standards are:

1 Safety.
2 Clinical and cost effectiveness.
3 Governance.
4 Patient focus.
5 Accessible and responsive care.
6 Care environment and amenities.
7 Public health.

All services are measured against these seven core standards, although not all aspects of every standard are wholly relevant to each service. For example, under Safety, psychological therapies are required to produce evidence that they are safe, with risk management policies and protocols, child protection training and adherence to NICE guidelines. Clinical supervision and clinical audit programmes in psychological therapies may provide evidence of clinical and cost effectiveness. Governance deals with how complaints are dealt with, and how records management policies and staff surveys are engaged. Patient focus measures choice, consent, confidentiality and patient safety. Accessible and responsive care requires evidence of patient involvement in planning, equity and choice and treatment not being discriminatory. Standard 6 is all about a healthy workplace within the NHS and a healthy setting for patient care. Standard 7 is public health, the work on whole populations, improving health, disease prevention and health promotion. This is an area where psychological therapies can raise their profile by providing evidence that their interventions contribute to public health targets from compliance with treatment to reduction in BMI or alcohol consumption.

What has changed for every service is the focus on numerical data and quantitative evidence. The NHS culture is driven by outcome frameworks and a robust evidence base. The services that can supply this information have an advantage and are embraced by commissioners. Other services may be as effective or even better, but unless they can provide the evidence to back up their claims, they will be left behind.

There are clear training and practice implications for counsellors. Levels of service activity, risk assessment, patient profiling, outcome frameworks and patient satisfaction surveys all have a place in a primary care service. Learning to work within time frames and to keep up with the administrative tasks and see the value of measurement is frequently seen as a hindrance to the real work with clients. But this is the real work of the NHS and the old style private practice model of professional autonomy is no longer relevant. However, professional judgement is a very necessary skill and learning to communicate with a wider primary care team yet preserve the boundaries of a confidential service is all part of the job. Part of the role of the service lead is to manage the boundary between the demands of the practitioner role and the demands of the primary care trust. Negotiating the balance between these two very different worlds is hard, especially as service leads are former clinicians and probably new to the leadership role.

The next document was *The National Service Framework for Mental Health* (NSF), published in 1999. The core values of the New NHS are enshrined in this document: service development, quality, equity and monitoring. Again there are seven standards, this time for mental health; five are specific to mental health provision and two (governance, and accessible and responsive care) are those included in the earlier document. The additional five are:

1 Mental health promotion.
2 Primary care and access to services.
3 Effective services for people with severe mental health problems.
4 Caring for carers.
5 Preventing suicide.

It is widely recognised that severe and enduring mental health problems have been the focus of service development in the first five years of the mental health NSF. The reorganisation of adult mental health services has required health and social services to work towards an integrated service with a focus on care outside hospital. So wards were closed as assertive outreach, crisis resolution, home treatment and early intervention teams were established.

Primary care services were directed by standard 2 to ensure that any service user who contacts their primary health care team with a common mental health problem should have their mental health needs identified and assessed and be offered effective treatments including referral to specialist services. Standard 3 said that an individual with a common mental health problem should be able to make contact round the clock with local services and receive adequate care, to include NHS Direct for first level advice and referral on to specialist help lines such as Samaritans. The NSF also directed primary care trusts to develop protocols for depression, anxiety, postnatal depression, eating disorders and schizophrenia. Examples of good practice and how standards could be achieved included the use of counselling and other psychological therapies focused on common mental health problems in primary care.

The NSF recognised that the majority of people with mental health issues (over 90 per cent) remained in primary care and that the bulk of the mental health grant is spent on providing services for a small percentage of the population. As the political momentum to reduce costs in the NHS by making services more efficient gathered force, policies emerged to redirect care from tertiary and secondary level services into primary care. This shift of resources into primary care is happening slowly. Primary care trusts are beginning to develop initiatives to bring services previously located in hospitals into the community. As with all change, there is resistance; for the hospitals there is little to gain as resources are being diverted elsewhere.

Directives followed (Appleby, 2004), one of which was to introduce 1000 graduate mental heath workers into primary care to work with common mental health problems, and using evidence-based interventions. In practice this has become supported self-help and signposting to other services. In general, these workers are relatively inexperienced and their introduction has raised more expectations than they could meet, given their level of training. Both the Sainsbury Centre and NHS Alliance have clearly stated that the role requires clarity and that their introduction has to be evaluated and assessed as well as appropriately supported. In contrast, gateway workers are professionally qualified mental health workers, with experience, who will support primary care teams to manage more serious problems within primary care without the need to refer into secondary care. As the name implies, they will manage the interface between primary care and community mental health resource centres. Always framed with an expectation that this is in the patients' and carers' best interests, nevertheless the assumption is that services will cost less and be more efficient.

There has been a mixed response to graduate workers, who are inexperienced and at the beginning of a career path. Psychologists were enthusiastic at first until they realised these workers were no longer just psychology graduates and were likely to be based in primary care and not in psychology departments. What graduate workers can do is support those with mild depression to use evidenced self-help packages and signpost to other services. This government-led initiative continues to uphold the myth that problems in primary care are simple and are easily dealt with by the least experienced workers. Any clinician in primary care knows that in the arena of mental health issues it is simply not possible or desirable for complex cases to be always referred to specialists in secondary or tertiary care. People refuse the offer of referral, preferring to stay in primary care where they are known; waiting lists are too long to be helpful and referral guidelines may exclude those outside defined diagnostic criteria. It is not surprising that GPs and patients were frequently confused and disappointed that graduate workers were not counsellors or therapists, could not undertake complex assessments and were not trained to offer counselling. Their introduction has begun a process of addressing complex need that has long been neglected. However, it is unrealistic to expect these graduate workers to meet such a longstanding shortfall in capacity.

The Sainsbury Centre for Mental Health (2002) made specific recommendations that graduate workers should be integrated into existing services in primary care, such as primary care counselling, where they could be supported and develop skills, assist with research as well as self-help and offer a valuable support role. This advice has not always been followed and an opportunity for more joined up thinking has been put on hold in some areas. In contrast, the gateway worker is an experienced mental health professional who offers support to primary care teams to ensure patients with serious mental health problems have their need met in primary care and that practices develop registers of patients with severe and enduring mental illness. Gateway workers have much to offer and if they develop skills in consultation and interagency working they will be especially useful. As with the graduate workers, role clarity is vital and their introduction will require evaluation and assessment. They too require good support. Again there was an assumption in these proposals that primary care was virgin territory when in fact psychological therapists from many disciplines had been working there for many years. The impetus had sprung from GPs recognising what worked and was popular with patients, although frequently these workers were isolated and not linked in with other services. There is also the trivial point that both these new posts began with a 'G'. Graduate worker or gateway worker? Who does what? The confusion continues and clarity through inter-disciplinary reflection time and clear patient pathways needs to be established. What is emerging is a recognition that all kinds of patients with complex needs are held in primary care and not always satisfactorily. The Sainsbury Centre (2005) has written a policy paper on the need for developing intermediate mental health care within primary care by bringing together existing staff with a special interest in this group who can form a specialist team to target what they call 'the neglected majority', using a stepped care approach.

The guidance, *Organising and Delivering Psychological Therapies*, was published by the Department of Health in July 2004. The intention was to provide an impetus to review psychological therapies and improve the delivery of services. The emphasis is on the need for coordination and consumer choice. This document crosses the divide between primary, secondary and tertiary care. The message is clear: psychological therapies are part of mainstream health care and there is plenty of evidence for their effectiveness in treating a wide variety of mental health problems. A lack of counselling and other psychological therapies is frequently cited by users and their families, when asked how they would like services to be improved. Access needs to be improved because there are frequently long waiting lists. The recommendations are practical: involve users more, establish a psychological therapies management team, and implement a stepped care approach to delivering psychological therapies. Training is vital because there is a huge need for a more psychologically literate workforce as well as increased psychotherapeutic skills in the development of new teams and services. One of the most useful aspects of this report is Appendix C, which lays out the framework for markers of best practice for managed services in the delivery of psychological therapies. Five levels of service for a clinical psychological therapy service are measured against benchmarks from 'not present' to 'beacon status'. The benchmarks are:

- targeting those in greatest need;
- that teams are multidisciplinary;
- evidence of a training strategy;
- single point of entry;
- involving users;
- a tiered network of service;
- managing waiting lists effectively;
- research and audit;
- clear defined leadership;
- supportive of a whole service that is psychologically minded.

Alongside these developments the National Institute for Clinical Excellence (NICE, 2004a, b) has published guidelines for treatment of depression and anxiety that are relevant to primary care mental health and psychological therapies in particular. Cognitive-behavioural therapy (CBT) is cited as the treatment of choice most frequently because this approach has more up-to-date studies available to demonstrate its effectiveness. Given the emphasis on 'evidence-based practice' this is not surprising. However, it was disappointing that the two guides on depression and anxiety suggest that CBT is always the treatment of choice without stating either that evidence from other modalities was not considered or that it was incomplete to guide treatment choice and therefore not endorsed. This bias was addressed in the NICE guidelines for the treatment of depression in children and young people and the fact the evidence base is not balanced was recognised. This means that psychological therapies and counselling in particular have to focus on research to improve the evidence base. Technology dominates the culture and the wish to find solutions dominates policy and service planning. The idea that time is needed to reflect and think is equated with doing nothing. What therapists have to do is demonstrate through outcome studies that helping people to reflect on their life, make connections and give meaning to their distress is of equal value to programmes to change thinking patterns and eradicate intrusive thoughts. Both approaches have a place and there is no 'one size fits all' approach when it comes to difficulties that have their origins in the human condition.

The Layard Report (2004) was presented to the Strategy Unit at 10 Downing Street. It has not been adopted as government policy yet but the findings are taken seriously by the Department of Health. This is an economists' view of the impact of mental illness on the economy (2 per cent of GDP). There are now more mentally ill people drawing Incapacity Benefit than there are unemployed people on Job Seeker's Allowance. The report makes the point that the majority of NHS resources for mental health go to the 1 per cent of the population with psychotic symptoms (severe and enduring) and there is very little left for those with depression and anxiety (mild to moderate) because of the lack of investment in psychological therapies.

Lord Layard suggests that clear objectives need to be set, with actions to achieve them. He thinks these problems can be solved, as there are not the same issues of recruitment that beset other parts of the health service. He has suggested training an additional 5000 psychological therapists and that the way forward is to set up specialist centres led by psychologists and psychiatrists. Given that these two professional groups are not in plentiful supply, there is a more cost-effective solution. Once again the fact that there are psychological therapists with years of training and experience working in primary care has been overlooked, namely primary care counsellors and psychotherapists. If patient choice is taken seriously, then the work has to be local in primary care teams. This has to be a cheaper option than the setting up of new centres.

The biggest change within the NHS is coming shortly and this is *patient-led commissioning*, also known as practice-based commissioning or local commissioning. Which term is used depends upon which document you read and who you talk to. How it will develop is uncertain and local solutions are likely to emerge in response to national directives. Definitive statements are premature because even basic issues like boundary changes will not be finalised until April 2006. It seems obvious that health, social services and education should have the same boundaries if they are to work together. Achieving this will be a major advance. The move to commissioning is to give patients a say in how services develop and for GPs to commission care on behalf of their patients. Primary care trusts will become the focus for public health, including health promotion and supporting the commissioning process.

The Chief Executive of the NHS caused consternation in July 2005 by announcing that PCTs would no longer be service providers from 2008. Although there have been soothing statements, which appear to backtrack on this, the overall policy is actually still in place. All services will be commissioned and psychological therapies, along with everyone else, have to prepare for commissioning by costing their service and having the evidence of their effectiveness. What the government wants to see is contestability: that is, the possibility of services being provided by outside agencies, which might be voluntary groups or private providers that already run hospitals or clinics. It may be that pharmaceutical companies will bid for services to run alongside pharmacies. The market place economy is enshrined in government thinking as promoting competition, encouraging innovation and service improvement, providing choice and keeping prices down. What are not discussed are the unintended consequences that always accompany changes. Will patients choose wisely? Do doctors want to spend their time on commissioning? Will not-for-profit organisations always offer best value? The one certainty is that savings will be less than predicted and expectations as well as services will have to be trimmed.

In this climate of uncertainty and change, watchful waiting is appropriate. The questions that require thinking about are: how will complex needs be met and joined up thinking in community service provision be developed? In every child protection inquiry following the tragic death of a child, included in the recommendations are that health, social services and education need to improve inter-agency communication. Professional communication is never easy and from assessments to care plans, they vary from a tick box mentality to a thoughtful enhancing experience for patients, carers and the staff involved. Professional communication across boundaries is even more difficult and requires training, practice and protocols. The 'silo' mentality persists, with no one taking into account the wider systems; and in times of change and turbulence, it becomes even more marked, with each professional group retreating and protecting known and familiar territory. Change in practice is resisted and developing new ways of working becomes unthinkable. Leadership has the task of containing the anxieties of staff sufficiently to allow them to get on with the day-to-day tasks and supporting them to think creatively and take on new ways of working. Clinical leaders too will feel under pressure and may react in predictable ways. One is to side with staff against the organisation, fuelling agitation and rebellion; the other is to become distanced from staff concerns and impose changes in an authoritarian manner that further alienates staff who may leave and plunge the service into rapid turnover and low morale. Holding the middle way requires huge support for clinical leaders and traditionally organisations have been slow to respond to the challenge, by providing not just training but ongoing support through supervision and learning sets.

The biggest threat in this brave new world is polarised thinking in whatever form it takes. Examples abound:

- the old ways are best and new plans are ill thought out;
- CBT is the only effective therapy and psychodynamic thinking is out of date and ineffective;
- PCTs are out of touch and only practices can commission in the interests of patients;

- patients always know what is in their best interest and health professionals must provide services patients want.

Everyone, in moments of stress, indulges in splitting into good and bad thinking; it is far harder to hold a balanced view, recognising shortcomings without blame and working to move things forward.

There is a fervent hope that commissioning will bring opportunities for service innovation and development and at the same time there is a threat of fragmentation if multiple providers are commissioned. How will training and development be protected as organisations compete to drive down costs? The government is very keen on the use of voluntary organisations, seeing them as a cheaper alternative. Voluntary counselling organisations frequently use trainees to offer counselling. This may be a good arrangement for both, because trainees gain experience and there are no staff costs; and counselling can be offered free or at very low cost, benefiting the community. Will PCTs support voluntary organisations to meet governance requirements? How can a spirit of collaboration and cooperation be fostered in a climate where organisations are competing for contracts? Will there be resources for the counselling organisation that employs qualified staff and offers career progression? Will there be career pathways for qualified counsellors or will they find that to earn a living they must work mainly in private practice?

Issues of equity have driven the service agenda over the past few years, and to see it abandoned in the move towards patient choice would be a retrograde step. There is a fine balance between diversity of provision and outright inequality. In the arena of psychological therapies and mental health, the challenge will be to commission services that protect the interests of the most vulnerable at the same time as meeting the needs of the majority. In this context, although training standards for primary care counsellors have been set and are widely recognised, what comes next is to recognise the need for management training for counselling services. Leadership skills are vital for the success of any project and these are not the same as clinical skills. Developing good leaders within clinical groups has been recognised as essential by the NHS but has yet to be fully embraced by psychological therapies, many of which are still grappling with operational issues.

The Emerging Relationship between Primary and Secondary Care

All of these actual and proposed changes mean that the boundaries between primary and secondary care are likely to become more fluid. Different structures and provision in different parts of the country make it hard to generalise. In some areas trusts are combined primary care and secondary mental health trusts, and in other areas primary care counselling is commissioned from the mental health trust. For many counsellors working in general practice it makes little difference which trust employs them. However, there are differences in the philosophy of care between primary and secondary care, which affect the relationship between the two. The strength of primary care is the focus on health and well-being, with an emphasis on prevention through immunisation and screening. It is accessed by the whole population and is largely free of stigma. Patients are known by name and over time at different stages of their lives. In secondary care the medical model is dominant, with an emphasis on diagnostic categories. What has happened in this period of rapid change is that mental health trusts have drawn their boundaries tighter, being much clearer about which people they will assess and support. Frequently these boundary decisions are based on diagnostic categories and anyone without a diagnosis of a moderate to severe condition is returned to primary care. This leaves primary care counsellors to see more patients with no increase in resources. Waiting lists grow and GPs become dissatisfied with both services, because no one is able to see the distressed patients quickly.

Traditionally counsellors in primary care have echoed their GP colleagues by becoming specialists in primary care and available to see anyone who is referred. Not that everyone is offered more than one session. But the philosophy is that any encounter can be used to good effect and has the potential to be therapeutic, be it one session or several. Counselling is particularly valuable for the common enduring mental health problems so familiar to primary care teams. These are particularly the patients who in another setting might be diagnosed as having a 'personality disorder'. They are known to primary care practitioners for their unreliability, frequent presentation of symptoms and mood swings. They often refuse offers to be referred on to specialists, preferring to remain where they are known. They will always need intermittent support. There is no quick fix solution but collaboration and cooperation between members of the team helps to mitigate the dramas and crises that beset these patients' lives. With the advent of commissioning and continuing scarce resources, will this philosophy continue? Perhaps it is time for primary care counselling to set tighter boundaries. What are its specialisms? Is it the management of complex cases requiring liaison with different services? Should primary care counselling do more to develop links with district nursing and health visiting to establish a service for those whose physical and emotional needs are intertwined with a chronic physical condition or whose mental health needs are bound up with the health of their children?

Good specialist training for counsellors working in primary care is essential. The standards developed so far provide strong foundations. Vigilance will be necessary to ensure these standards are protected and promoted as new models of service emerge through commissioning. The therapeutic skills practised by counsellors have proved their worth, both in helping patients and in supporting inter-professional dialogue. The next phase will require work to ensure they survive and are recognised as a valuable contribution to primary care mental health.

Commissioning and Core Standards

To sum up, a beginning has been made in the setting of standards for primary care counselling. The context of primary care is evolving at a rapid rate and there will be an increasing need for psychological therapies to be part of primary care. Commissioning brings with it opportunities for service development as well as problems of fragmentation. Key to the whole process will be the development of primary care mental health strategies.

These have to reflect the philosophy of primary care, with its emphasis on health and well-being rather than disease and dependence. Partnerships with the voluntary sector are essential to deliver patient-centred care for the twenty-first century. Primary care counselling has to decide whether it remains an optional add on and likely to be commissioned from a variety of sources; or part of an integrated primary care team working in collaboration with other agencies towards a seamless interface with children's services, adult mental heath services and services for the elderly. The field is wide open!

References

Appleby, L. (2004) *The National Service Framework for Mental Health Five Years on*. London: Department of Health.

Balint, M. (1957) *The Doctor, His Patient and the Illness*. London: Pitman.

Department of Health (1997) *The New NHS: Modern, Dependable*. London: HMSO.

Department of Health (1999) *National Service Framework for Mental Health: Modern Standards and Service Models*. London: HMSO.

Department of Health (2004) *Organising and Delivering Psychological Therapies*. London: HMSO.

Department of Health (2005) *Commissioning a Patient-led NHS*. Briefing Document to Chief Executives of NHS Organisations.

Layard, Lord R. (2004) *Mental Health: Britain's Biggest Social Problem?* (available from www.strategy.gov.uk/downloads/files/mh_layard. pdf).

National Institute for Clinical Excellence (2004a) *Management of Depression in Primary and Secondary Care*. London: NICE.

National Institute for Clinical Excellence (2004b) *Management of Anxiety in Primary and Secondary Care*. London: NICE.

Sainsbury Centre for Mental Health (2002) *Primary Solutions Briefing 19*. London: SCMH.

Sainsbury Centre for Mental Health (2005) *The Neglected Majority: Developing Intermediate Mental Health Care in Primary Care*. London: SCMH.

Summary

What Now?

Douglas Hooper and Philippa Weitz

There have been some very recurrent and consistent themes throughout the book. These views, promulgated by a wide variety of authors and the national organisations that they represent, have to date rarely been translated into good practice. The reader who has now read right through the chapters that we have assembled will have a clear idea that two things have happened over the past years, namely:

1 A significant group of mental health workers practising psychological therapies has become established. These people are often called 'counsellors' because this is the basic training for many of them. In the Agenda for Change that is now in progress throughout the NHS, the category of 'counsellor' has been explicitly recognised in employment terms at three levels of expertise. There are now probably 2000–3000 practitioners at work in primary care working with a wide variety of patient problems.

2 The amount of competent specialist training for these practitioners has lagged far behind the employment of these same practitioners because of a lack of training resources, both people and funding, despite a very well worked out programme that has been not only taught in some centres but also widely disseminated by the Couselling and Psychotherapy Forum for Primary Care and practitioner groups, and NHS manager practitioners.

We can confidently expect that over the next few years mental health issues in the community will receive significantly more attention than in the past years, which could be accompanied by enhanced funding for this sector. Yet the government has been very unwilling to accept and adopt the current significant practitioner body to take forward the expansion in services that are necessary. Instead it (or its advisors) has looked to develop quite new services such as the 1000 psychological assistants who will derive from sources other than the normal counsellor training programmes.

We have to ask ourselves why the government has been so unwilling to work with the current counsellors. It is a short answer: counselling in primary care grew out of the counselling movement and was and is not the result of a government directive. We see the newly arrived graduate mental health worker as coming from a completely different stable: it is a Department of Health initiative and as such receives all the infrastructure and money that goes with that.

Nevertheless, despite all the odds counselling in primary care has survived its difficult, underfunded and undervalued origins to take its place alongside other psychological therapies. It has also achieved formal employment recognition as we mentioned above.

We can now say that today, with Layard's new thinking about the economics of mental health and visionary ideas put forward in the Sainsbury Centre for Mental Health's (2006) *The Future of*

Mental Health: A Vision for 2015, that the opportunities for the primary care counsellor have never been better. However, they will need to be adaptable, and perhaps be pragmatic at times. For example, we wonder at the tunnel vision of the pursuit of cognitive-behavioural therapy as the therapy of choice. Translating that into drug terms, it would be a bit like saying that only one anti-depressant will be offered to patients – when the reality is that we know that some work better than others and that it takes clinical skill to get the medication right. In the world of psychological therapies we have such a broad range of treatment options available, and the evidence supports the view that the therapeutic alliance rather than any specific approach is the most important aspect of patients' recovery.

At present there are already a significant number of different professionals active in the mental health field, and it seems foolish to create yet more different professional groupings. Instead, the financial and personnel resource should surely be focused on those practitioner groups already in place and doing the job. It could be argued, of course, that the problem at present is that those practitioners are *not* doing the job (of managing psychosocial distress) effectively or efficiently. This has been said but there is little or no evidence to support the contention. What certainly *can* be said is that developments in psychological therapeutic practice have not been adopted as widely as might have been hoped for, particularly in the realm of active work like cognitive-behavioural therapy. But the rational approach is surely not to develop yet another practice group but to ensure that resources are provided for practitioners to widen their repertoire of skills.

The early investments in counselling in primary care made by the Counselling in Primary Care Trust in the development of the early MAs have proved beyond reasonable doubt that when people are well trained they go on to do great things. So the bottom line is to finance training and service delivery. There has been little or no public funding of counselling in primary care training, its clinical survival has been dependent on some creative accounting (one of the authors was once listed as a cleaner for payment purposes!) and none of the recommendations made in this book by some very heavyweight authors (together with the organisations they represent) will see the light of day unless the Department of Health and the government is behind the profession.

In the counselling in primary care profession there is already a dedicated and largely very well trained workforce ready to rise to the challenge required to ensure that the vision for mental health in 2015 will be achieved. We therefore urge our readers to action. Don't just stand there, do something! If the argument of the book is persuasive (as we believe it is), then current practitioners, managers and teachers need to make their voices heard in both professional and political spheres. The need of the 25 per cent of attendees presenting psychosocial difficulties at GP surgeries throughout the UK is too important to allow partial or half-baked solutions to emerge when other coherent paths are available and known to be effective.

Reference

Sainsbury Centre for Mental Health (2006) *The Future of Mental Health: A Vision for 2015*. London: SCMH.

Appendices

For electronic versions of all Appendices, please go to the resources section on <www.karnacbooks.com>

APPENDIX 1

Counselling and Psychotherapy for Primary Care Forum Membership

BACP	British Association for Counselling and Psychotherapy
BPS	The British Psychological Society (Counselling Psychology Division)
CPC	Association of Counsellors and Psychotherapists in Primary Care
CPCT	Counselling in Primary Care Trust
RELATE	Relate – the Relationship People
QCA	Qualifications and Curriculum Authority
SMG	SMG Professional Risks (and conference sponsors)
UKATC	United Kingdom Association of Therapeutic Counsellors
UKCP	United Kingdom Council for Psychotherapy

APPENDIX 2

Minimum Training Standards for Primary Care Counsellors

1 Introduction

1.1 The Counselling and Psychotherapy Forum for Primary Care (known hereafter as the Forum) was set up in 1999 by a number of interested parties. Professor Douglas Hooper is the Chairman. Its membership is listed in Appendix 1.

1.2 The members of the Forum came together with a joint purpose, which was to address the diverse nature of training for primary care counsellors. The overall aim of the Forum is to set quality, standards and excellence for education, training and professional development of counsellors, psychotherapists and psychologists working in primary care.

1.3 It is up to the individual professional member organisations to adopt and implement these standards.

1.4 Ultimately, the concern of Forum members is that the care offered to clients and patients is of the highest standard. The Forum believes that care is based on sound research, and that practitioners should be able to communicate in a professional way with their primary care employers and their fellow care workers. The Forum believes that setting the minimum set of criteria for clinical academic and clinical training underpins all else and that the setting for the provision of primary care counselling is what defines it.

1.5 Prior to its formation some of the major parties met with a view to developing understanding and common causes. This group ran a consultation day in April 1999 and a conference in November 1999. Training organisations were particularly invited and represented. The Forum grew out of these meetings and events.

1.6 The use of the term 'primary care counselling' (sometimes shortened to 'counselling' in this document) is used as a short hand for all the psychological therapies used in primary care, including counselling, psychotherapy and psychology. It is the setting that determines the term.

1.7 Its policy development is concerned with the delivery of quality psychological services in primary health care.

1.8 The Forum has undertaken extensive discussions and consultation in this area. It sees its role as that of setting minimum training standards and of providing expertise and advice to interested parties about training for counselling in primary care.

1.9 This document is one result of a training mapping exercise examining the content of training courses and a needs analysis for primary care counsellors, which was completed in spring 2001.

2 Generic Training Requirements

2.1 Primary care counselling is a more skilled task than that most initial diploma courses prepare students for. This is because of the range of patients seen and the brief therapy utilised. The Forum wishes to emphasise the central importance of development of the trainee's capacity to create and sustain an appropriate therapeutic alliance.

2.2 Time is required for students to consolidate reflective practice and benefit from the developmental nature of counselling training. Consequently, a professional, generic counselling/psychotherapy training needs to be undertaken over a substantial period and provide the necessary theoretical, clinical and experiential components.

2.3 Selection

2.3.1 The selection of students on to such counselling and psychotherapy courses whether delivered in training institutions or academic institutions needs to evaluate the psychological availability of the candidate for the training ahead as well as their educational, work experience and personal qualifications. Rigorous procedures for all components of selection need to be in place and monitored. Further selection for suitability for training in primary care is also necessary. The Forum will shortly be able to provide guidelines as to selection criteria and procedures.

2.4 Assessment

2.4.1 Criteria and procedures for the assessment of competency are needed for ongoing assessment during training and on completion of training.

2.5 Personal therapy

2.5.1 Personal therapy is a requirement for training in counselling and psychotherapy in primary care for the following reasons:

- It allows the practitioner the opportunity to explore their unconscious reasons for undertaking this training/work.
- It enables the practitioner to experience and understand the process of examining their internal world in relation to another, before asking it of patients.
- It allows for the working through of the practitioner's

own psychological material which may otherwise impede the work with patients.

- It gives the practitioner the opportunity to understand, develop and monitor safe practice and the centrality of therapeutic boundaries.
- It is expected that practitioners will continue to monitor their psychological health after the training therapy has been completed and undertake further personal therapy through the process of their professional life as and when required or desirable.
- It is recommended that practitioners only enter into contracts with patients of the frequency experienced by the practitioner as a patient/trainee/client undergoing therapy.

2.6 Models of Training

2.6.1 Two models of training are considered particularly appropriate:

- A minimum of 3 years generic counselling/ psychotherapy training plus a minimum of 1 year post qualification for primary care counselling training.
- A 4-year training, which includes all requirements. The final year would introduce a brief/focal model or demonstrate how the taught model is applied in a brief/focal way.

2.7 Generic Trainings

2.7.1 The expectation is that generic trainings will include:

- Psychiatric/mental health assessment.
- Risk assessment and assessment skills.
- Management of practice.
- Ethical and legal issues.
- Knowledge of mental illness.
- Sexual issues.

2.7.2 We consider that the therapeutic alliance is a critical factor in counselling, and understand it to be an essential component of all trainings.

3 Primary Care Specific Trainings

3.1 Training for primary care counselling needs additionally to be context specific, and to prepare trainees to work competently in a time limited way. There may be a number of routes to achieve this.

3.2 The Forum is proposing a minimum standard, and is aware there are some excellent courses, which exceed this minimum. Requirements for primary care specific trainings are:

- Psychotropic drugs/medication
- Primary health care team relationships
- NHS structure
- Assessment particularly when working to a time limit
- Knowledge of mental health referral pathways and procedures
- Brief focused therapy methods

3.3 Trainings will take into account the need to fit the theoretical model respectfully to the patient, rather than the other way around.

3.4 We would recommend in all training, and require for primary care training, input on:

- Interactive processes in families
- Systemic theory
- Audit and evaluation methodologies

4 Supervision

4.1 The Forum recognises the key role that supervisors play in the development of trainees' and practitioners' practice.

4.2 The following principles have been agreed:

4.2.1 Supervision must be relevant to primary care.

4.2.2 The training supervisor should have specific knowledge or experience of primary care counselling, and of brief focused therapy.

4.2.3 The training should include an agreed number of supervised clinical hours with a ratio of 1 hour of supervision to 6 hours clinical practice and with flexibility to increase the ratio for the beginning practitioner, at the discretion of the supervisor.

5 Mentoring

5.1 The Forum recommends that clinical placements for trainees in primary care are best offered only under the guidance of a mentor, and where the practice has a standard commensurate with that of a training practice.

5.2 The mentor must be an experienced practice counsellor working in that practice or in another practice that can accommodate the work undertaken by the mentor.

5.3 The provision of mentoring is distinct from clinical supervision and involves various essential components such as: assessment of suitable patients, teaching, training and management of the placement.

6 Clinical Accountability During Placements

6.1 The Forum recommends that clear and written agreements as to clinical accountability for the student's work should be made between the GP Surgery, the Training Supervisor, the Mentor and the Training Institution.

7 Remit of the Forum Regarding Training Standards

7.1 It is envisaged that this document provided by the Forum will help applicants choose suitable courses for the training of primary care counsellors, and help course and placement providers to review their provision.

APPENDIX 3

Person Specification Criteria for Primary Care Counsellors

Background

This protocol has been put together by the Counselling and Psychotherapy Forum for Primary Care after much consultation with training organisations, counsellors, supervisors and service providers.

It is intended to provide a framework for all parties to adhere to in the lead up to statutory registration and to be nationally adopted as the 'acceptable standard'.

For **employers** and **service managers** it will provide clear guidance of the qualities, training and expertise required by counsellors working within primary care.

For **students/trainees and trained counsellors** it provides a framework of training that you need to achieve for competency to work in primary care.

This document should be read and used in conjunction with the **Minimum Training Standards Protocol**, also produced by the Counselling and Psychotherapy Forum for Primary Care.

Definition

A counsellor in primary care here refers to the setting of the work, not the initial training of the therapist. We recognise that counsellors in primary care come from a wide diversity and richness of backgrounds and do not have a homogenous initial training.

What makes a well-trained counsellor in primary care stand out is that he or she will have fulfilled the person specification criteria.

Person Specification Protocol for Counsellors in Primary Care

Aim

To define the training, placement, personal therapy, service and supervision standards for a primary care counsellor.

This document is relevant for:

- NHS commissioning managers/human resources;
- NHS counselling service managers;
- trainers providing courses for those seeking employment in the NHS;
- counsellors considering employment in the NHS.

Implementation of the recommendations in this document will result in quality counselling provision in the NHS and fulfil clinical governance requirements.

Initial Generic Counselling Training

450 hours:

- core theoretical model(s);
- skills training.

This level of counselling training needs to be acceptable to the relevant professional bodies and will also lead to accreditation/ registration with BACP/CPC.

It is suggested that training courses, which prepare people for work in the NHS, include:

- assessment (including mental health and risk management);
- ethical frameworks for professional practice;
- general legal issues;
- working with diversity;
- 40 hours minimum on personal development (this means individual personal therapy);
- 100 hours minimum on managed and supervised clinical placement.

Specialist Counselling Training

In addition to the above, those seeking employment within the NHS need to include in their continuing professional development (CPD):

- NHS structure and policy;
- clinical governance;
- NHS multidisciplinary working;
- knowledge of mental health referral pathways and procedures;
- psychotropic medication;
- focused, evidence-based practice;
- time-limited therapy;
- audit, evaluation and research;
- notes/confidentiality and the law.

This may be acquired through taught CPD modules and/or clinical experience, validated by critical reflection and professional portfolio developments.

Student and Post-Qualification Placement Guidance

Placements

Guidelines for students and post-qualification placements are available from the professional bodies. These require management, mentoring and supervision. The student would expect a negotiated placement.

Professional Counselling Service Standards

- Mentoring – for students or newly qualified practitioners.
- Induction – for newly appointed practitioners.
- Appropriate management of the service and the practitioners.
- Clinical counselling supervision – an ethical requirement of all professional counselling bodies.
- Quality assurance – evidence of audits, evaluation and research based practice.

Counselling Supervisor Requirements

- postgraduate qualification in counselling supervision;
- knowledge of NHS structures/policies and counselling practice;
- meets clinical governance requirements.

Counselling Manager Requirements

A counselling practitioner with knowledge of:

- NHS structures/policies;
- a professional counselling perspective;
- management expertise;
- knowledge of audit, evaluation, research, training and supervision.

The 1995 Course Proposal

Core Module 1: Working within a Multidisciplinary Team in the NHS

Knowledge: Counsellors need to know and keep up to date with the rapidly changing structures and funding of the Health Service, to understand how primary care fits with secondary care, and with provision for mental health and mental illness. They need to understand the medical model. They need to know how to create appropriate structures for referral and confidentiality.

They need to learn how to work in a different way and manage waiting lists for counselling, if necessary, in a setting where medical staff expect to respond immediately to all requests for service.

A developed knowledge of elements of effective teamwork is also necessary.

Skills: Counsellors need skills that are seldom explicitly taught on counselling courses to contribute to effective teamwork. This includes assertiveness skills to ensure clarity of communication, and negotiating and co-working skills to enhance the coordination of service to patients.

Awareness: An understanding of the dynamics of groups and teams, both conscious and unconscious can prepare the counsellor to contribute to formal or informal consultancy to team members.

Core Module 2: Models of Health and Illness

Knowledge: Counsellors in primary care need an up-to-date basic knowledge about psychopharmacology, and of mental illness (6, 7, 8), to work collaboratively with the medical team. They also need to know about specific psychosocial implications of diseases commonly managed in primary care, and have information about resources to extend that knowledge as clients come forward with less common diseases. Particular topics such as eating disorders, and sexuality are important.

Skills: Counsellors need to extend their skills and awareness of health counselling and lifestyle counselling approaches (9), and to consider family, couple and group work options for responding to patients with new, chronic or terminal diagnoses, with chronic pain and so on.

Awareness: They need to review their assumptions about health and illness. In particular, they need to develop their understanding of familial and cultural assumptions and trans-generational patterns of illness, and how other cultures and subcultures might construe symptoms differently (10). They also need to increase their awareness of their attitudes to medical colleagues.

Core Module 3: Models of Time Effective Therapy

All counsellors in primary care are being pressed to work preferentially within a brief therapy model where a norm is four to six sessions, and the routine range is between single sessions and a maximum of ten in any one series. Yet few counsellors have training in brief therapy methods.

Knowledge: Counsellors need a structured opportunity to review the brief therapy models, and assess how far the assumptions fit with their own. They need to explore the bases in cognitive-behavioural ideas, and 'solution focus' or 'possibility focus' paradigms, and develop their own models of time effective work which fit with and extend the way they practise, and match the setting.

Skills: Most time effective therapies are present and future focused rather than past focused, and rely on proposing homework tasks, giving compliments to clients to reinforce their awareness of their strengths, use of imagery and imagination to identify desired goals and so on. Whichever model the counsellor chooses to apply they need to develop the skills associated with that model.

Awareness: Counsellors need to explore the possibilities and limits of new paradigms, and where they feel comfortable or not in applying them. It is important to give time to integrating the new knowledge and skills with the established working methods, which serve them well already as experienced practitioners.

Core Module 4: Personal and Professional Development

The Counselling in Primary Care package invited students to reflect on their personal and professional self care in the personal and professional development element. An aim for the future was to offer this material also to form the basis of a module for a staff team to study together.

The module had six components:

- Self-assessment materials.
- Integrating theory and method.
- Confidentiality, power, and appropriate contracts.
- Practice issues: caseload/workload management.
- Professional/personal review.
- Supervision.
- Attending to transcultural issues.

Example of Self-assessment Material. Caring for the Carer: Strategies for Self-care

It was and is apparent that many practitioners in the health care system suffer from stress. They resort to inappropriate strategies to continue work under highly stressful circumstances, and are at risk of premature burnout. Counsellors are not exempt from internal and external pressures, and need to be taught strategies to anticipate and manage their own stress where possible. The BACP ethical framework now puts this as an essential element of ethical practice.

The syllabus for this included:

- The development of an understanding of the structure, organisational context and culture of the workplace, and the impact on the individual practitioner of role conflict and role strain.

- An exploration of the practitioner's motivation to do the work.
- An exploration of their capacity to focus and set appropriate boundaries.
- Identification of their own network for personal support, and whether they feel they have an appropriate balance of satisfactions in their lives.
- An awareness of their personal style and how well it fits with those of dominant others in the team.
- Learning to monitor their energy levels and developing understanding of positive stress management.
- Use of supervision to sustain well-being.

APPENDIX 5

Useful Website Addresses

British Association for Counselling and Psychotherapy	www.bacp.co.uk
British Psychoanalytic Council	www.bps.org.uk
British Psychological Society	www.bps.org.uk
CORE (Clinical Outcomes for Routine Evaluation)	www.coreims.co.uk
Counsellors and Psychotherapists in Primary Care	www.cpc-online.co.uk
Organising and Delivering Psychological Therapies	www.dh.gov.uk
National Service Framework for Mental Health, Modern Standards and Service Models	www.dh.gov.uk/nsf/mental
Agenda for Change	www.dh.gov.uk/policyandguidance/humanresourcesandtraining/modernisingpay/agendaforchange/fs/en

Department of Health NHS Site www.doh.gov.uk

Adult Mental Health Services: Final Report by the Workforce Action Team, Special Report (Appendix C, p. 27) www.doh.gov.uk/nsf/mentalhealth.htm

Counselling and Psychotherapy Central Awarding Body (CPCAB) www.info@cpcab.co.uk

ENTO www.ento.co.uk

Faculty for Healthcare Counsellors and Psychotherapists (BACP) www.fhcp.co.uk

The Healthcare Commission www.healthcarecommission.org.uk

Health Professions Council www.hpc-uk.org

National Institute for Clinical Excellence www.nice.org.uk

Professional Associations Research Network www.parn.org.uk

Quality Assurance Agency for Higher Education www.qaa.ac.uk

Qualifications and Curriculum Authority www.qca.org.uk

United Kingdom Council for Psychotherapy www.psychotherapy.org.uk

Sainsbury Centre for Mental Health www.scmh.org.uk

Layard Report, Mental Health: Britain's Biggest Social Problem? www.strategy.gov.uk/downloads/files/mh_layard.pdf

National Profiles for Clinical Psychologists, Psychotherapists and Counsellors www.wise.nhs.uk/sites/workforce/retaininganddevelopingstaff/Document%20Library151/1/Allied% 20Health%20Professions/Clinical%20Psychologists,%20Counsellors%20and%20Psychotherapists.pdf (See Appendix 6)

APPENDIX 6

National Profiles for Clinical Psychologists, Psychotherapists and Counsellors

Can be found on resources section on <www.karnacbooks.com>

INDEX

Page numbers in *italics* refer to tables, *n* indicates endnote, *a* indicates appendix, *passim* refers to numerous scattered mentions within page range.